Silent Sisters

Profiles of the short lives of

KAREN CARPENTER
PATSY CLINE
CASS ELLIOT
RUBY ELZY
JANIS JOPLIN *and*
SELENA QUINTANILLA-PEREZ

Ellen Hunter Ulken

Cover Design by Eric Ulken

Table of Contents

The music in my heart I bore,
Long after it was heard no more

—William Wordsworth (1840-1932)

Art is not a mirror held up to reality
but a hammer with which to shape it.

Bertolt Brecht (1898-1956)

For Eric and Bénédicte

For my mother, Phyllis

For Jerry

Introduction to 'Silent Sisters'

I grew up singing American songs, everything from Stephen Foster's "Oh! Susanna," to "Grandfather's Clock," by H.C. Work. Our family moved around a lot, but popular music was always a constant in my young life. In seventh grade, at DuPont Junior High near Fort Lewis, Washington, I earned my music letter with "Seven Lonely Days," trying out my untrained voice on the mostly empty classroom.

During high school in Jasper, Florida, my friends and I came out of the Faye Theater humming tunes from *Gigi*, *The King and I* and *High Society*. Thanks to Jimmy Biddle, we had culture in Jasper. Mr. Biddle owned and operated the Faye Theatre, the only "picture show" in town. Much of what we young people anticipated and admired was projected onto the screen at the Faye. Cartoons, serials and movies, both dramatic and musical, dazzled our imaginations and revealed a world beyond tobacco fields, pine forests, country lanes and little town monotony.

We heard Theresa Brewer, The McGuire Sisters, Perry Como and Dean Martin crooning their magic over the radio while we cruised around town in our parents' cars.

Soon, the radio rocked as Little Richard blasted out the lyrics to "Good Golly, Miss Molly!" The voice of Elvis thrummed with "Heartbreak Hotel," and from there, the music world rattled and rolled into the future. We found thrills on Fats Domino's Blueberry Hill and danced to the music of Ray Charles, who grew up in my corner of the Florida woods.

It seemed to me–a teenager of the fifties–that this new, outrageous music with a beat had arrived to stir up the atmosphere of our ordinary little town, and startle my generation into a wider world we would soon enter as adults.

I began writing in middle age and discovered that playing with words on a page gave me pleasure. Because I admired and appreciated his songs, and because there's a memorial to him in Hamilton County, where I hail from in Florida, I wrote a short biography of Stephen Collins Foster, the first American popular songwriter of the 1800s.

For my next writing effort, though I admired the work of Irving Berlin and George Gershwin, who followed in Foster's footsteps, I wanted to study and honor a woman. Trying to match the achievement of someone like Gershwin, who died young, (as did Foster) I searched for a musically accomplished woman who would be a worthy subject for my next book. She didn't have to be a composer but she had to have made a contribution to the great flow of American music. Like Foster and Gershwin, she would have had a short life. I found six singers who fit the profile.

In the late 50s and early 60s, while in nurse's training in an Atlanta hospital, I lost track of popular music. Within that cloistered environment death existed both as an enemy and a reality. I developed an awe of death through an early contemplation of it. Premature loss of life still stuns me. "She was robbed," I think to myself when someone's life is snuffed out before she has reached her three score and ten.

Death at a young age is always tragic. But is the finality of it assuaged for artists who leave behind a body of work? For the women of this book—Karen Carpenter, Patsy Cline, Cass Elliot, Ruby Elzy, Janis Joplin, and Selena Quintanilla-Perez—their voices live on in the recordings that survive them.

While indulging my love for American music and history, I set out to discover these talented ladies: Who were they? What compelled them? How did these singers achieve so much within so few years? What did they have in common? Why did they die too soon?

All were born into musical families. All plowed through personal and professional barriers along their journeys. All had enormous talent, the determination to succeed, and the courage to sing and perform unabashedly before an audience. They laughed, made friends easily, and collaborated with fellow musicians to perfect their craft and propel themselves to stardom. On stage, when the curtain swished open, they rose to glory.

When the curtain closed and time came to engage in the real world, personal challenges confronted them. They toured relentlessly. Each suffered the consequences of grueling schedules, back-to-back performances, travel weariness, and the confinement and monotony of the road. This worrisome commonality prompted another question: Could tight schedules and exhaustion be implicated in the anxieties and dramas that surrounded their early deaths?

This book weaves together respectful snapshots of their journeys on and off the road. In the process, the pages recall and celebrate a great many American songs, which the now *Silent Sisters* performed to resounding success.

Karen Carpenter in performance at the Royal Festival Hall, London in 1974. (Tim Graham/Getty Images)

Karen Carpenter   (1950 – 1983)

On the last evening of her life, Karen talked by phone with her friend Phil Ramone about an album they made together. They agreed that even though it hadn't been released to the public, the album was "freakin'-great." Karen had dinner with her mother and father at Big Boy's restaurant and ate a shrimp salad, her favorite. She watched a taped episode of "Shogun," starring Richard Chamberlain with her parents at their home and stayed overnight there in her brother's old room.

At midnight, she telephoned her girlfriend, Frenda, to confirm their plans for the following day; first Karen wanted to shop locally for some new laundry machines, then she and Frenda would meet at the manicurist's and have bright red polish painted on their nails to celebrate Karen's divorce that day. From there they would go to the lawyer's office to sign the final papers. Karen told Frenda that she felt tired–her chest felt tired–and Frenda called downstairs to suggest that Karen's mom, Agnes, check on her. When she did, Agnes covered Karen with a blanket and thought she seemed all right.

Next morning Karen came downstairs to the kitchen, turned on the coffee maker, set the table for two–just for her parents–and returned to the bedroom. Once Agnes heard Karen stirring, she went to the kitchen to prepare cereal and called upstairs to tell Karen the coffee had perked. No answer. Agnes climbed the stairs to find her lifeless daughter face down on the closet floor.

When Karen Carpenter was born in New Haven, Connecticut on March 2, 1950, her brother Richard was three-and-a-half years old. Their parents, Agnes and Harold owned their home and wanted the best for their children. Agnes confronted problems and situations in an assertive manner, while Harold seemed more easy-going.

Harold loved beautiful cars and in addition to Harold's job as a printer, the couple ran a car-cleaning business to earn extra cash.

Agnes and Harold adored Perry Como, Bing Crosby, big bands and pop songs. Harold collected stacks of the old 45 and 78-rpm records for his family's entertainment, and listened attentively while Agnes sang along with the invisible crooners.

Richard remembered playing a Fred Waring recording of "Over There" so many times that the hole in the middle of the record wore out. Richard also admired Frankie Laine's "Mule Train," and Theresa Brewer's "Music! Music! Music!" Listening closely to the arrangements for overtones and shadings, he studied every style variation and memorized the sounds.

When Richard was seven and Karen was four, he sang along with the lyrics floating out of the records, in the basement of the New Haven house. Karen sang too, glad to be in the company of her big brother, but she showed more interest in pitching a baseball, jumping rope, playing with her toy gun, or with Snoopy, the family dog.

The Carpenter kids frolicked daily with the neighborhood children. Karen, more outgoing than her brother, defended Richard against any bullies that came around. Bright-eyed and chubby cheeked, Karen seemed happy in her world.

Richard lived for music. His piano teacher, Hank Will, encouraged his precocious talent, taught him piano and theory until he was thirteen, and then directed him to the Yale Music School.

Hank came around so often that he became part of the family. Agnes and Harold had raised their niece, Joanie, from infancy. When Karen was born, Joanie was already a teenager. By the time Karen reached her teens, Hank and Joanie had fallen in love and they married in 1963.

In the summer of that year, leaving the newlyweds behind, Harold and Agnes moved the family to Los Angeles, trading snowy winters for eternal summer. Harold hated the Connecticut winters, and the couple felt certain that Los Angeles would offer greater opportunities for their gifted son.

They lived in Downey, a commuter suburb of Los Angeles on the edge of Orange County, and soon owned a house. Harold worked as a skilled pressman and Agnes got a job at North American Aviation Company. The Carpenters counted every dollar and taught the children thrift by example.

Richard settled into the local music world through church and school as a performer and teacher of piano. He brought Jim Squeglia to the Carpenter's home for jam sessions. A drummer and a member of Richard's music group at school, Jim remembers that Karen watched and admired his drum playing, but at 13, she didn't display her brother's passion for music. In her school autobiography she wrote that she liked to dance, collect records and draw. She expected to become an artist or a nurse.

When Karen entered high school, Physical Education class was mandatory unless you played in the band. Karen didn't like running track, so Richard asked the band director to let Karen join the band to keep her out of P.E. Since she didn't play an instrument, the director gave her a glockenspiel. While marching with the bells in the Downey High School band, Karen kept an eye on the drummers, particularly the talented Frankie Chavez. Intrigued and beguiled by the drums, she begged her Mom and Dad for a set.

Frankie Chavez helped the family choose a set of Ludwigs, and Karen learned to play Dave Brubeck's "Take Five" and "It's a Raggy Waltz." Frankie taught her basic concepts and gave her tips. She later studied technique with Bill Douglass in Hollywood.

In high school, Karen also joined an all girls' band, Two Plus Two. "Ticket to Ride," a Beatles song, was one of their favorite pieces. Karen's talent astonished the band director, who always thought of drums as instruments for men only.

Jerry Vance, a schoolmate of Karen's, escorted her to school dances, but she preferred her drums to any boyfriends.

Karen had been drumming on her own for some months when she began working with Richard and Wes Jacobs.* They practiced often together at the Carpenter home, where Agnes, who encouraged the musical sessions, always supplied a mixture of iced tea and lemonade for the group. By spring 1965, Richard, Wes and Karen had gigs at weddings and restaurants, billing themselves as The Richard Carpenter Trio.

Frank Pooler, Richard's voice teacher at California State University, Long Beach, gave Karen singing lessons while she was still in high school. "Her range was spectacular," [1] recalled Pooler, and her voice ripened with his guidance.

In May of 1966 Richard invited Karen to go with him to Joe Osborne's studio for a midnight recording session. Osborne, a bassist who played for big name bands such as The Mamas and the Papas, had a makeshift studio in his garage lined with cork and egg cartons to keep the sound down. Karen went along for fun, not expecting to sing. But she did sing, and when they replayed the recording the magic in her voice struck Richard like a blast of fresh air.

With Karen drumming (not singing), The Richard Carpenter Trio won best combo at the "Seventh Annual Battle of the Bands" at the Hollywood Bowl. They played " Iced Tea," Richard's jazz waltz composition, and Richard's arrangement of "The Girl from Ipanema." Richard also took the outstanding instrumentalist award. And they won the sweepstakes trophy for highest score. Richard was nineteen, and Karen, sixteen.

---

* Wes Jacobs went on to study at The Juilliard School and then to play Tuba for many seasons with the Detroit Symphony Orchestra.

By this time Richard had met John Bettis, a fellow music student at CSU, Long Beach. Richard was proper, straight and tailored compared to John's scruffy long hair, old coat and boots. Richard liked pop songs with a choral background, while John preferred folk music. Together they crooned in harmony and wrote songs. Without Karen, who was still in high school, Richard and John hired other musicians to play with them. They called themselves "Summerchimes," then "Spectra," and then "Spectrum." They practiced at the Carpenter home five days a week. Still, the recording studios rejected their music, due to the lack of rock and folk in the repertoire. They sounded good but not "cool." Eventually John Bettis quit the band, but he and Richard would write many songs together over the years to come.

In the spring of 1967, Karen graduated from Downey High School, winning the John Philips Sousa Band Award, the highest honor for high school band students.

In the fall, Karen enrolled at California State University, Long Beach, where she was already studying voice. After the weekly sessions with Frank Pooler, Richard drove her to drum lessons.

At 145 pounds, Karen was a bit chubby. She went on the Stillman diet that year and lost 25 pounds. To her shimmering dark hair, sparkling eyes and perfect skin, she added a slim figure.

In the summer of 1968, after Spectrum dissolved, Richard decided to concentrate on his trio, which included Karen, Bill Sissyoev, a bassist, and himself. Richard trusted that with the right sound and the right song, recognition would soon be theirs. Sure enough, as *Carpenters,* they won first prize on television's, "Your All American College Show."

One of their taped recordings found its way to the office of Herb Alpert. "When I heard Karen's voice I was charmed," said Alpert of Tijuana Brass fame. "It was love at first hear." [2]

17

He signed the Carpenters for A&M Records, with a $10,000 advance and seven percent royalties. Karen was 19-years old and her parents had to cosign with her.

Rock music dominated the music scene and the Carpenters didn't fit the mold. Singing ballads and love songs, the pair "took showers and got haircuts" as Karen would say defensively, and wore turtlenecks and velvet costumes. Alpert's colleagues ridiculed him for investing in the duo, but Alpert, a trumpeter and singer himself, admired their superb musicianship.

In 1969, Karen and Richard performed for two film premiers, "Goodbye Mr. Chips," and "Hello Dolly." The Carpenter's album, *Offering*, didn't soar to fame but "Ticket to Ride," released as a single from the recording, climbed to number 54 on Billboard Magazine's charts.

Karen took her role as Richard's partner seriously. Punctual for practices, she took little leisure time and her college courses didn't get much attention. Except for music courses, Richard's classes lagged as well. They went from rehearsals to gigs and back to rehearsals.

Richard arranged their music to Karen's vocal strengths, choosing the right songs for her range and highlighting her mellow alto voice. Her low notes enchanted listeners. As she would later say, "The money's in the basement."

A succession of boyfriends pursued Karen, but work came first. She would cancel a date without hesitation if Richard called her for a rehearsal.

Alpert liked "Close to You," a song by Hal David and Bert Bacharach and thought it would be perfect for the Carpenters. He encouraged Richard to add extra musicians to find the right sound for it. The recording of "Close to You," climbed from number 56 to the top of Billboard's charts, and stayed there for four weeks, selling a million copies. "Close to You," the Carpenters all-time best hit, set them soaring.

"We've Only Just Begun" stemmed from a bank commercial that Richard liked and thought ideal for Karen. Roger Nichols and Paul Williams made a song of it at Richard's request. "We've Only Just Begun" sold a million and a half copies and became their signature number.

The Carpenters music was everywhere, a soothing contrast to the clang and crash of pop rock. Their success was instant and explosive.

Money flowed into their bank accounts and for $300,000 they bought a new house for the family on Newville Street in South Downey.

In 1970, they won Grammy awards as Best New Artist and Best Contemporary Vocal Group. "Close to You," the album and the single, respectively, won nominations for Album of the Year and Record of the Year.

On a rare night off while on tour, the Carpenters went to the movies. When they heard the ballad from the wedding scene in *Lovers and Other Strangers*, Richard decided to record it. "For All We Know" sold over half a million copies, becoming their third Gold record.

"Rainy Days and Mondays" written by Paul Williams and Roger Nichols, became their fourth best seller. "They made great records," said Williams. "They took our songs and gave them a life." [3]

In May of 1971, The Carpenters performed at Carnegie Hall to rave reviews. Cousin Joanie and Hank Will lived nearby and threw a party for them afterward.

"Superstar" by Leon Russell and Bonnie Bramlett debuted in 1971. Richard first heard Bette Midler sing it on Johnnie Carson's TV show and wanted it for Karen, who rendered it superbly on the first take.

From 1970 to 1975, five arduous years, Richard and Karen took their show on the road. They traveled cross-country and internationally, sometimes doing one-night stands and taking time off only to come back to Los Angeles to rehearse, record, or do something for television. The schedule wore them out physically and emotionally as they pushed to meet expectations of fans and to keep their stars flying high. For the lack of managers arranging time to rest, the young performers kept a relentless pace.

Richard later acknowledged that they should have been recording instead of "flogging around" on tour. Touring Britain and Japan were necessary but they would have had more music available and earned more money if they had stayed at home and made records.

The roadies came by the Newville house to pick up Karen's costumes. Karen packed her stage outfits into a huge trunk she nicknamed "Blackula." The crew would slide the trunk down the stairs to load it into a van that took it to the large trucks, which carried the sound and stage equipment to the next performance place.

The Carpenters and their entourage routinely rose early, traveled to the next city by bus or by plane, had lunch, played a rehearsal, went to the hotel to shower and dress, and on to the venue for the performances and autographs, then dinner, sleep, and more of the same the next day, and the next–a peripatetic existence.

A factor that accompanied their life on the road was the restricted company they kept. If romance bloomed, it grew from within the group because they had little opportunity meet anyone else. When Richard dated Maria Galliazzi, Karen's hairdresser and wardrobe manager, Karen erupted. Maria was HER hairdresser, and she didn't approve. She and Agnes broke up the romance. Hopelessly in love with Richard, but realizing his family entanglements, Maria quit her job.

Karen felt secure and safe behind the drums, loving her instruments, and knowing she played them well. Singing seemed like a sideline to her. But after three hits Richard convinced her that her vocals embodied the focus of the band's appeal, and that she would have to stand closer to the audience. For the ballads, then, she came to the front mike, and when the music called for drums she took her usual place behind them. In a later interview Karen related the fear she felt when standing out in front to sing.

"There was nothing to hold on to, nothing to hide behind." [4] She had loved drumming and singing at the same time.

"My drums, by this time I had so many of them all you could see were my bangs." [5] She didn't ask to be "the star," and didn't really want that. The family revered Richard and considered him the great talent. Karen wanted nothing to do with detracting from Richard's fame. Later, she made a needlepoint piece for him, and on it she sewed. "There's no K.C. without R.C."

Paul White, the road manager, became friend and confidant to Karen. Sometimes she rode in the truck with him when they traveled from town to town. He encouraged her as she adjusted to her new role as lead singer. Richard didn't intrude into Karen's private life as readily as she did into his, but when Sherwin Bash wanted to fire Paul, Richard agreed. Paul had been her guide. She missed him when he left.

Richard hired Jim Squeglia to play the drums when Karen sang. Richard didn't allow improvisation. Jim had to play the drums like Karen played them and just as they sounded on albums. Though the salary was good, Jim felt frustrated by the lack of artistic freedom on stage. Jim gave Karen an occasional hug during rehearsals, thereby clashing with Sherwin Bash. Bash feared romance. Soon, by mutual agreement, Jim left the group.

Cubby O'Brien, a former Mousketeer, replaced Jim Squeglia on drums. While growing up, Karen had watched the Mickey Mouse Club on TV. She adored the famous Mickey, and admired O'Brien's Mousketeer history.

Other band members included Gary Sims, Doug Strawn, Bob Messenger and Danny Woodhams, all versatile, accomplished musicians.

Firmly grounded within his sphere of music, Richard led and collaborated with an ardent purpose. Karen took his direction eagerly. Their teamwork was a fine-tuned instrument and the essence of their success. Luck had little to do with their triumph.

Karen and Richard expected perfection. They never erred, though Karen would sometimes second-guess, "...maybe, I could have done it better." [6] The entire band had to be technically correct.

"You couldn't fake it," [7] said Tony Peluso, a guitarist. If a band member made a mistake during a performance, they heard about it from one of the Carpenters. Band members played for Karen and Richard's approval, and not for public applause.

Loyalty lodged in the sibling's souls. They shared profits, friendship and the stage with fellow musicians, and took bows together. Sometimes, after the shows, they socialized as a group. If Karen and Richard flew first class to the venue, so did the others. All rode together in limos. All had private rooms at hotels. And later when the group broke up, the Carpenters provided generous severance packages. Karen, especially, strove to please everyone: fellow performers, family members, company officials and friends.

Tony Peluso played an electric guitar solo on the recording "Goodbye to Love," breaking an artistic barrier. Allowing the guitar riff to be featured within the song was something new. The record soared to number seven, and the inclusion of a solo riff in the middle of a song was, thereafter, widely imitated by others.

Their recording of "Sing," from Sesame Street, came out in February of 1973, sold a million records, and won two Grammy nominations.

Three months later Richard Nixon invited the Carpenters to perform at the White House during a state visit from Willy Brandt, Chancellor of West Germany. Exhausted and in the middle of a tour, they arrived at the White House with the entire band. Karen recalled being nervous, playing and singing in the East Room, a smaller hall than they were used to. She felt challenged to play the drums softly, in deference to the distinguished guests. Nixon, a musician himself, had become a true fan and referred to the Carpenters as "young America at its best." [8]

"Gute Nacht," said Karen to Chancellor Brandt, as the concert ended, "Auf Wiedersehen."

They next recorded a couple of songs which Richard Carpenter and John Bettis had written over two days time. The first, the title song for *Now and Then*, "Yesterday Once More," rose to number two on the charts. The other grew out of a comment that Bettis made upon discovering that the Carpenters sometimes traveled from town to town aboard private Lear jets.

"Wow, you're really on top of the world," [9] he said. When the song came out, the Carpenters were indeed at the peak of their fame, in song and in life. "On Top of the World," with a country twang, made it to number one in the USA and to number five in Britain.

John Bettis said that though they composed and crooned songs of love, their love lives–Richard's, Karen's and his own– were unfulfilled. Unless romance happened to blossom within the troupe, they stayed too busy with careers to find love or even to look for it. The longing and melancholia in Karen's singing voice reflected the emptiness in her own life. She wanted to marry and loved children.

In spite of meteoric record sales and soaring admiration from fans, jeers from critics about their music not being "hip," bothered them. "Goody four-shoes," and "squeaky clean" they heard again and again. But the Carpenters stood firm in their musical style. Their melodies recalled the past, reached for the future, closed the generation gap, and enthralled the entire spectrum of music lovers, young and old.

For Karen, an occasional comment in the tabloids about her appearance hurt deeply and may have triggered her obsession with a sense that her looks didn't meet expectations.

For six years, Karen's weight had remained a steady 120 pounds. She was a 23-year-old pretty young woman with dancing brown eyes and a fine figure, when, on a publicity picture of herself, Karen thought she noticed some extra flesh. She started exercising. She didn't like the muscles that resulted from the exercise, so she quit working out in late 1973, and began dieting.

When the siblings weren't on the road, they lived with their parents. In 1974, Karen and Richard bought a new house on Lubec Street in Downey, ostensibly for their parents but the folks wanted to stay at their old place, so brother and sister took the new house.

Richard's girlfriend at that time was their manager, Sherwin's daughter, Randy Bash. When Richard wanted to move Randy into the new house, Karen balked. She and Agnes again disrupted Richard's personal life. Still, the romance lasted many months despite disapproval from Agnes and Karen.

Richard liked *Les Paul and Mary Ford* and emulated their overdubbing techniques. Karen and Richard both admired *The Beach Boys*, the music of Burt Bacharach, and *The Beatles*.

Richard collected vintage cars and Karen collected Mickey Mouse paraphernalia. Karen didn't read much but she liked to watch TV and do needlepoint. She sewed a wall hanging for her parents, a picture of a yellow street with a green dollar sign at its end, and the words "You Put Us On The Road." But time for hobbies was limited.

1974 brought two more hits. "I Won't Last a Day Without You," and "Please, Mr. Postman."

The Carpenters had and still have as many fans in Japan and Britain as in the United States, and they toured both countries to sell-out crowds. The Japanese, who like melody instead of the dissonance so prevalent in modern music, wanted to hear the Carpenters. And in London the duo played the world-class Palladium to enthusiastic audiences.

On tour, band members noticed that Karen didn't appear at meals, which historically they had all shared. When she lost 5 pounds, Richard told her she looked good and didn't need to lose any more weight. At this point, if Karen had gotten some intensive treatment, perhaps the tragic downward spiral of her illness could have been aborted. But family and friends were mystified by her eating behaviors, since so little was known about Anorexia Nervosa at the time. The pounds kept dropping off. She drank thin soups and ate small salads without dressing or half a scoop of ice cream, once a favorite.

In 1975 Karen met Terry Ellis, probably the love of her life. Karen always felt that the man she married should be successful in his own right. Ellis was. He owned half of "Chrysalis," a profitable British record company. But he liked to go out for long, gourmet dinners and Karen preferred stay-at-home suppers in front of the TV.

Richard got along well with Ellis, both professionally and socially. Both were wine lovers. And Richard took Ellis' advice on some business matters including, "Get a new manager." When Bash was fired, Ellis ran the Carpenters, temporarily.

Ellis felt that their record company hadn't been sufficiently attentive to Richard and Karen. He began to teach Karen the rudiments of stagecraft, which he thought A&M* should have long before accomplished.

---

* A&M Records also had an operation in Britain, where Carpenters' music was in great demand. Sales of Carpenters' records brought money to the company, helping to fund the popular—but less profitable—rock groups of the period.

By 1975 Karen's ribs showed beneath her skin. Audiences gasped at the sight of her. At 80 pounds she didn't have the energy to complete the grueling world tour for which they were scheduled.

Resting at home under Agnes's care, she gained 24 pounds and read fan mail from all over the world. The letters soothed and consoled her.

Once better, Karen vacationed with Ellis in the Virgin Islands, and then moved in with him in Los Angeles, but Agnes didn't approve of "living together," and by then Karen was in the clutches of her anorexia. The divergent mealtime lifestyles didn't help. Karen moved out, and Ellis moved on.

Agnes erupted in anger when her daughter announced her intention to buy her own condominium. But Karen went ahead with her plan. She adored her new home, and decorated it with Mickey Mouse and Disney pieces, some that she collected and others that fans sent her; but Karen was abidingly loyal, and even after she moved into her place on Avenue of the Stars in Century City, she drove back to Downey to visit her parents, sometimes staying overnight.

In her spacious condo with its lovely view of Los Angeles, she organized the closets perfectly with pants all together and blouses side by side. Her doorbell chimed the first notes of "We've Only Just Begun." The refrigerator stayed empty, as did the kitchen cupboards. When she ate out, she gave her food away.

A new manager, Jerry Weintraub, negotiated a better deal with A&M Records, including higher royalties. Weintraub also encouraged the Carpenters to try television. They appeared as guests on *The Ed Sullivan Show*, *The Perry Como Show*, *The Bob Hope Show*, and hosted their own TV specials.

A Christmas program brought them enormous success and ran again during subsequent holiday seasons. Years earlier Frank Pooler had written "Merry Christmas Darling." When Richard wanted a fresh Christmas tune, he wrote new music to Pooler's words, creating a perfect song for Karen's voice. And Karen sang "Santa Clause is Coming to Town," like a lullaby. Listening to the CD, you can picture her cozy on the sofa, cuddling a few little ones around her, gently crooning the song.

Throughout 1975 and 1976, Karen and Richard continued to record hits. By 1976 Richard had developed a problem with prescription sleeping pills, and by September of 1978 his physical condition had so deteriorated that he needed in-patient treatment as well as months of relaxation before he could work again.

The Carpenters played their last live show together at MGM Grand in Las Vegas, cutting short their tour. Richard let the band go, thinking the break would be temporary, and went for treatment in Topeka.

Karen flew to London to fulfill a performance contract. The band members, like affectionate brothers, encouraged Karen to eat and gain weight. She picked at her food and drank water with lemon juice. She had dropped to a size two.*

Richard encouraged his sister to seek in-patient treatment, but she wanted to make a solo album. Seeing Karen's

---

* Theories about anorexia nervosa have evolved since Karen suffered. Studies reveal that there is a genetic component to the disease. Anorexics tend to be perfectionists. In addition to the biological implications, social and psychological problems co-exist to inflict the disease. Anorexics come to the illness each from a different place, and a patient's treatment must address his/her individuality. No longer is poor parenting blamed for the victim's starvation. She feels in control when she begins to diet—ninety percent of anorexics are female—but at some point she loses it, and her life becomes an obsession with eating, purging rituals. Early intervention improves the chance of recovery.

determination, Richard gave his blessing for her to work with Phil Ramone in New York.

One of her old boyfriends David Alley, who once ran their sound systems and now worked as a personal assistant to the Carpenters, took her to the airport for her flight. David had always been in love with Karen and though she felt an abiding affection for him, she saw him as a friend. David could have been a good husband for Karen but as a member of the Carpenter work team, he didn't satisfy her notion of a suitable marriage partner. She was booked on an L1011 for the trip. Jittery, she preferred 747s but David encouraged her to board the 1011, assuring her it was a safe ship.

With the move to New York to do the solo album, Karen declared her independence. Good friends with Ramone's fiancé Karen Ichiuji, who Karen called "Itchy," Karen lived with the couple in a suburb of New York and drove with Ramone daily to the city for work.

Karen loved singing on her own and trying something new, but she was used to Richard's direction. Ramone challenged her. He had her singing intimate songs with sexual overtones, and while her voice seemed good, she lacked stamina. "Itchy" and Ramone noticed Karen's predictable trips to the bathroom after meals. One night she collapsed and they had to call the paramedics.

In the end the album wasn't released. "Not good enough," said the bosses at A&M records.*

Back in Los Angeles, living in her beloved Century City condo, she contacted her old boyfriend Terry Ellis, hoping to start over. To her crushing disappointment, Terry told her he was engaged to marry someone else.

Richard was ready to go back to the studio but Karen looked so thin, he wouldn't work with her. Again, she moved

---

* The CD of Karen's solo New York recording, *Karen Carpenter*, was released in 1996.

in with her parents. With the help of a Beverly Hills specialist and under Agnes' care, she got up to 106 pounds. Harold told Karen that if she didn't take better care of herself she wouldn't be around much longer.

Karen kept her beautiful voice and her keen sense of fun. She sent postcards and presents to pals, including "Itchy" Ramone, Carol Curb, and Olivia Newton John. "Olivia was affectionately referred to as Livvy or ONJ (which Karen pronounced Ahhnj.)" [10] Dionne Warwick, Petula Clark and Frenda Leffler were also among her friends. Karen was the Godmother to Frenda's twins. Awaiting the twins' birth, Karen was nearly as excited as the parents. Named Ashley and Andrew, Karen called them "the kidlets."

She had great camaraderie with company managers and band members. She called Sherwin Bash, "Shermine Bush." Their accountant, Werner Wolfen, she named, "W." For "W"'s office, she crafted a needlepoint wall hanging: TANSTAAFL, their private acronym for, "There ain't no such thing as a free lunch."

She adored Lucille Ball and *I Love Lucy*, and traveled with the Lucy tapes so that she could watch them on the road. Karen could be droll and funny herself, and often she would pretend to be "Lucy" to her girlfriends' "Ethel." She hoped for a role in a musical comedy.

Karen yearned for a fairytale prince, and when she met Tom Burris, a seemingly successful businessman, on a blind date arranged by her friend Carol Curb, this charming man became part of her dream. On August 31, 1980 after a whirlwind romance with Burris, they married in lavish splendor at the Beverly Hills Hotel. Flowers and music filled the halls and "Because We Are In Love, (The Wedding Song)"–composed by Richard Carpenter and John Bettis–rang through the halls.

With tears in his eyes, Karen's old friend, David Alley stood with the guests. Still employed as a personal assistant to the

Carpenters, he had made the arrangements for Tom and Karen's wedding trip to Bora Bora, holding plane tickets in his pocket.

The newlyweds came home early. Bora Bora was "boring, boring," [11] said Karen. Their room had no TV.

For a few months, she seemed happy to friends. She wanted children and had chosen names. A little boy would be named for Richard, and be called Rick or Richie. A daughter would be named Kristi*.

A few days before the wedding, Tom told Karen that he wasn't able to have children. Crushed and miserable, Karen wanted out but Agnes thought it was too late to cancel. Invitations had been sent. Guests were coming from the East Coast and London. A fortune had been spent. Though Tom had offered to have a reversal of his vasectomy, it isn't known whether he made good on the offer. Other disappointments followed.

Sadly, one year and three months after the wedding, following Harold's 73rd birthday party in Downey, Tom Burris left his wife at home with her parents. "You can keep her," [12] he said to Agnes and Harold, and drove away.

Cousin Joanie was visiting at the time. She hugged and consoled Karen through that night as she sobbed and grieved the severance of her ties to Tom.

The failed marriage threw Karen into turmoil. "I'm just afraid that I'm gonna miss it all,"[13] she would soon confess to her therapist. One song, her favorite of all the songs the Carpenters had recorded–"I Need to Be in Love,"–expressed her fear of having wasted too much time on her career without achieving her deepest goals: a solid marriage and children.

It was November 1981, and weighing 78 pounds, Karen flew to New York for a year of outpatient therapy with Steven

---

* Richard and his wife Mary would name their first daughter Kristi in Karen's honor.

Levenkron, an eating disorder specialist. She lived in a suite at the Regency Hotel and walked the 19 blocks to the therapist's office five days a week for one-hour sessions. By this time she was taking up to ninety tablets daily of the laxative, Ducolax, as well as overdoses of thyroid hormone. During twelve years of treating anorexics, the therapist had never before heard of a patient taking thyroid hormone as a metabolism accelerator. He took the thyroid pills away from her but she continued taking laxatives.

Karen renewed her ties with childhood friends and neighbors in Connecticut and saw them on weekends. "Itchie" Ramon stayed close. Dennis Heath, a friend since college, came to see her, as did John Bettis. She sent visitors away from her suite by 9:30 p.m., saying she had important phone calls to make, and spoke daily with her mother by telephone.

In October 1982, a frantic Karen called Levonkron. She felt dizzy and her heart beat a strange rhythm. Levonkron arranged a hospital admission through an M.D. associate. Since Karen's digestive system was damaged, nutrition was provided by hyper-alimentation—an intravenous feeding method through a large central vein—which didn't require her to eat. She gained 30 pounds. Tragically, the extra weight strained her weakened heart.

Richard came to New York to visit her in the hospital, hoping to see improvement; but he was discouraged by Karen's gaunt appearance. He told her that the treatment had failed, otherwise she wouldn't be in the hospital, and that she needed to try other tactics.

Gradually, she began to eat regular meals. In November 1982, one month after the hospitalization, Karen pronounced herself well enough to return to Los Angeles.

As a thank you gift, she sewed a calligraphic needlepoint piece for her therapist, which read "You Win, I Gain," and returned to California in time for Thanksgiving.

She drove her red Jaguar home to Downey for frequent visits. Though she bubbled around energetically during the day, she was tired at night, and on occasion felt her heart pounding. Richard noticed that there was no life in her big brown eyes. When he told her she didn't look well, she became angry and assured her brother that she was gaining weight, that she was better.

Florine Elie, the family housekeeper who worked for Agnes and Harold, came once a week to clean Karen's condominium. She once found Karen asleep in her walk-in closet, sprawled on the floor there. As she woke up, Karen said, "I am just so tired." [14] Florine helped her to bed, covered her, and called later to check on her.

Karen performed publicly for the last time on December 17, 1982. She sang Christmas songs for her godchildren, Ashley and Andrew Leffler and their schoolmates at the Buckley School in Sherman Oaks, California. Wearing red slacks and a colorful holiday sweater, she was happy that day. "She loved singing more than anything in the world," [15] said Frenda Leffler.

She wanted to work, and she and Richard were meeting with their production manager to talk about doing a concert. A comeback album had shown promise.

But on February 4, 1983, Karen collapsed at her parent's home in Downey and couldn't be revived. Emetine cardio-toxicity, heart failure, anorexia nervosa, and cachexia were listed as causes of death.

Ipecac syrup (emetine) is poison to the heart. The drug is kept in medicine cabinets to induce vomiting in emergencies, but should never be used otherwise. The autopsy indicated that sometime in the past she had used ipecac regularly and that it had damaged her heart. Cachexia described her weakened, debilitated state.

Almost 33 years old, she would have signed divorce papers had she lived six hours more. Instead, Tom Burris tossed his wedding ring into her casket.

A legal will protected most of Karen's assets, naming Agnes, Harold and Richard as her main beneficiaries.

Over 1000 mourners came by The Downey Methodist Church to say goodbye. During life, Karen feared burial and had shared this fear with friends. "She pleaded that she never be 'planted.'" [16] The term 'planted' was Karen's humorous reference to the unwanted ritual of interment into the earth. To honor the wish, her body was put to rest above the ground in a mausoleum at Forest Lawn Memorial Park in Cypress, a suburb of Los Angeles. "A Star on Earth, A Star in Heaven," is inscribed upon her monument. Years later, Richard had her remains and those of Agnes and Harold re-interred within a mausoleum at Valley Oaks Memorial Park in Westlake Village, CA.

Karen's tragic death brought anorexia nervosa and bulimia into the national spotlight. The Carpenter family founded The Karen A. Carpenter Memorial Foundation to conduct research on eating disorders and to discover effective treatments. They set up a memorial scholarship fund for music students at CSU, Long Beach. The memorial fund, now called the Carpenter Family Foundation, is a perpetual source of financial funding for causes ranging from medical to arts and entertainment to education.

In June 1983, Dennis Heath, Richard Carpenter and John Bettis performed a concert tribute to Karen with the California State University Choir conducted by Frank Pooler.

On October 12, 1983 Richard was present for the dedication of their star–The Carpenters–on the Hollywood Walk of Fame, at 6931 Hollywood Boulevard near the corner of Orange Avenue.

Herb Alpert wrote "Song for Karen," and dedicated his 1983 album to her.

In 1984, Richard married Mary Rudolph at the Methodist Church in Downey. Their union produced several children. With album releases, Richard has kept the music of the Carpenters alive, and through the recordings, Karen's magical voice lives on.

Opposite: The Carpenter Mausoleum, Valley Oaks Memorial Park, Westlake Village, California

Below: The Richard and Karen Carpenter Performing Arts Center, California State University in Long Beach. The lobby contains a small museum, which includes a collection of Gold Records, a display of other awards and photos and a set of Karen's drums.

Karen Carpenter
Bibliography:

Coleman, Ray, *The Carpenters, The Untold Story*, Harper Collins, New York NY: 1994

Levonkron, Steven, *Treating and Overcoming Anorexia Nervosa*, Charles Scribner and Sons, New York: 1982

Lucas, Alexander, *Demystifying Anorexia Nervosa*, Oxford University Press, New York NY: 2008

Rumny, Avis, *Dying to Please: Anorexia, Treatment and Recovery* second edition, McFarland and Company Inc. Publishers, Jefferson, NC: 2009

Schmidt, Randy L. *Little Girl Blue: The Life of Karen Carpenter* Chicago Review Press, Chicago Illinois: 2010

Schmidt, Randy, *Yesterday Once More: Memories of the Carpenters and Their Music*, Tiny Ripple Books, Cranberry PA: 2000

Stockdale, Tom. *They Died Too Young, Karen Carpenter*, Chelsea House Publishers, Malaysia: 2000.

Whitburn, Joel, *Top Pop Singles 1955-1993*, Menomonee Falls, Wisconsin: Record Research Inc., 1994.

Quotes:
1 "Her range was spectacular." – Schmidt, Randy *Little Girl Blue* Page 42

2 "When I heard..." *Close to You Remembering the Carpenters: The Story of Karen and Richard Carpenter and the Songs that made them famous.* DVD

3 "They took our songs..." *Close to You Remembering the Carpenters: The Story of Karen and Richard Carpenter and the Songs that made them famous.* DVD

4 "There was nothing..."Schmidt, Randy *Little Girl Blue* Page 86

5 "My drums, by this time..." Schmidt, Randy *Little Girl Blue* Page 86

6 "...maybe, I could..." Coleman, Ray *The Carpenters: The Untold Story* Page 155

7   "You couldn't fake..." Coleman, Ray *The Carpenters: The Untold Story* Page 139

8   "young America at..." Coleman, Ray *The Carpenters: The Untold Story* Page 143

9   "Wow, you're really..." Coleman, Ray *The Carpenters: The Untold Story*

10   "Olivia was affectionately..." Schmidt, Randy *Little Girl Blue* Page 154

11   "boring, boring," Coleman, Ray *The Carpenters: The Untold Story* Page 284

12   "You can keep..." Coleman, Ray *The Carpenters: The Untold Story* Page 291

13   "I'm just afraid..." Coleman, Ray *The Carpenters: The Untold Story* Page 312

14   "I am just so..." Schmidt, Randy, *Little Girl Blue* Page 272

15   "She loved singing..." Schmidt, Randy *Little Girl Blue* Page 270

16   "She pleaded that she never be..." Schmidt, Randy, *Little Girl Blue* Page 288

More Notes – Karen Carpenter

Page 13. - On the last evening – Page 274, *Little Girl Blue*, Randy Schmidt, from here out referred to as Schmidt
    At midnight – Page 275 – Schmidt
    Next morning – Page 275 – ibid
    Climbed the stairs – Page 276 Schmidt
    By the time...Karen Anne was born – Page 35 *The Carpenters The Untold Story*, Ray Coleman, from here out referred to as Coleman.
Page 14. - "Harold was a lover of beautiful cars..." – Page 33 – Coleman
    Agnes and Harold listening and singing– Page 35 – ibid
    "Over There" – Page 35 – ibid
    Teresa Brewer – Page 38 - ibid
    Richard lived for music – Pages 40 and 41 – Coleman
Page 15. - Move to Los Angeles – Pages 48 and 49 – ibid
    Harold and Agnes jobs – Page 49 – ibid
    Karen watched and admired – Page 44 – ibid
    In her autobiography – Page 47 – Coleman
    Glockenspiel – Page 52 – ibid
    Dave Brubeck – Page 52 – ibid
Page 16. - Jerry Vance, boyfriend – Page 55 – ibid
Page 17. - the spring of 1967 (graduation from Downey High School)– Page 37 – Schmidt
Page 18. - "...the money's in the basement." – Page 237 – Coleman
Page 19. - Carnegie Hall – Page 79 – Schmidt

37

Page 19. - "Superstar" – Page 105 – Coleman
Page 20. - Richard later acknowledged – Page 138 – Coleman
        The roadies and "Blackula" – Page 161 – Schmidt
Page 22. - Loyalty and friendship – Page 119 – Coleman
        "Sing" from Sesame Street – Page 128 – Coleman
Page 26. - Agnes erupted – Page 206 – Coleman
        Karen adored her new home – Page 208 – ibid
Page 27. - Footnote – The genetic component and perfectionism – Page 35 *Dying to Please* – 2nd Edition – Avis Rumney
        Also in Footnote – No longer is poor parenting blamed – Introduction, Page XVI – *Desmytifying Anorexia Nervosa* – Alexander R. Lucas. M.D.
Page 28. - She was never to be booked – Page 261 – Coleman
        Drove with Ramone – Page 265 – Coleman
        Paramedics – Page 268 – ibid
        With the help of a specialist – Page 279 – ibid
        Harold told Karen – Page 257 – ibid
Page 29. - TANSTAAFL – Page 325 – Coleman
        She adored Lucille Ball – Page 206 – Schmidt
        With tears in his eyes, David Alley – Page 284 – Coleman
Page 30. - Wedding – too late to cancel – Pages 226 and 227 – Schmidt
        Cousin Joanie – Page 291 – Coleman
Page 31. - Ducolax and thyroid – Page 293 – Coleman
Page 32. - Florine Elie – Page 272 – Schmidt
        December 17 performance – Page 270 – Schmidt
Page 32. - Causes of death, Ipecac.. – Page 283 and 284 - Schmidt

Discography:

Carpenters A&M Records, Hollywood, CA 1971
Carpenters - Interpretations, a 25th Anniversary Celebration: A&M Records, Hollywood, CA 1995
Carpenters The Essential Collection 1963-1997 A&M Records Santa Monica, CA: 2002
Karen Carpenter A&M Records Hollywood, CA 1996

Videography:

Carpenters Gold, Greatest Hits, Santa Monica, CA: A&M Records 1985.
Close To You, Remembering The Carpenters, The Story of Karen and Richard Carpenter and the Songs That Made Them Famous, VS Productions, MPI Home Video: 1998.
This is Your Life Ultimate Collection: Disc 3 Ralph Edwards hosts: The Carpenters and others, Ralph Edwards Productions: 2005

Patsy Cline circa 1960, Michael Ochs Archives/Getty Images.

Patsy Cline (1932 – 1963)

"I want to yodel," said Patsy to Owen Bradley, "I'm a country girl, and proud of it."

"Oh no, Patsy," said Bradley. "No more yodeling,"[1] Owen Bradley ran the Nashville office for Decca Records. He worked with Patsy for years, guiding and training her. Patsy and Bradley argued but he usually kept the upper hand. He encouraged Patsy to sing in a more popular style, and didn't want to hear any country overtones.

"Owen Bradley and Patsy Cline had much in common."[2] Both Patsy and Bradley had grown up poor and quit school in their middle teens to find jobs to help support their families. As kids, both had listened to big bands by the hour over the radio. Bradley concentrated on the sounds of the instruments, especially the piano. Patsy memorized the lyrics of the songs crooned by the vocalists.

Virginia Patterson Hensley, who became known to the world as Patsy Cline, was born in Winchester, Virginia on September 8, 1932. Her family called her "Ginny." Her mother, Hilda, age 16, was a seamstress; her father, Sam, a 43-year-old blacksmith, had been a soldier in World War One. For the first months of Ginny's life, Hilda managed on her own with the baby, living in a shack on her in-laws' farm, while Sam left town for work.

At age four, little Ginny saw a Shirley Temple movie and imitated her steps, dancing over the whole house. She won first prize in a tap dancing contest without ever having a single lesson. Later, when she heard her half-sister Temple Glen,* playing the piano, she wanted to learn the instrument.

The Hensleys' fortune ebbed and flowed but during the five years between Ginny's fifth and tenth years, they had a stable home life in the vicinity of Washington and Lee University in Lexington, Virginia, while Sam worked as a maintenance person for the University. Their house, near campus, was fully equipped with kitchen, bath, running water and electricity. Ginny attended the local elementary school for three consecutive years. The Hensleys bought a radio and a used piano. Ginny played by ear such songs as "The Old Rugged Cross" on the upright piano. From her bedroom window, Ginny could hear live music from the bands playing for the University dances: The Dorsey Brothers, Benny Goodman, Eddy Duchin, Woody Herman—all the greats.

Other than this brief respite from poverty, the family moved eighteen times during Ginny's childhood, from one small Virginia community to another—from Winchester to Gore to Elkton and back to Winchester—to wherever Sam could find work. And sometimes their abodes were primitive, without water and electricity. Fortunately, Hilda was a resourceful mother. She fished the rivers and grew vegetables in her back yards to add food to their cupboards.

Sam Hensley had a beautiful tenor voice. On Saturdays the family listened to the Grand Ole Opry over the radio and sang along. Hilda said she encouraged her daughter to sing because the singing didn't cost them anything. Ginny's greatest ambition was to become a member of the Opry.

---

* Sam had been married once before. His first wife died in a car crash. By this marriage, there were two children: Temple Glen and Randolph. After their mother died, these children were raised, and when Sam lost interest in them, eventually adopted by their music teacher. Sometimes Patsy would visit her half sister, an accomplished pianist, in this separate music filled household.

She suffered a throat infection at age thirteen and had to go under an oxygen tent. She floated in and out of consciousness, nearly lost her life, and later claimed that from the time of her recovery, she had "a voice that boomed forth like Kate Smith's." [3]

From childhood, she knew she was special. Described as a standout in school, she was sassy and assertive. Some classmates didn't like her because they saw her as pushy. In her lifetime, she never got the respect of the Winchester "upperclass" and she resented the way she was treated by the hometown folks. They ignored her and sometimes booed her. Later in life she would say, "One of these days, I'm going to come to Winchester and draw one hell of a crowd." [4]

Ginny Hensley made her radio debut at her hometown radio station at age fourteen, with more pluck than polish. Disc jockey Joltin' Jim McCoy and his band played live on WINC radio in Winchester on Saturday mornings. Ginny asked him point-blank if she could sing on the show. Jim figured if she had enough courage to ask, he had enough courage to place her behind the mike.

At age fifteen, Ginny, her mother Hilda, her brother, eight-year-old Sam Jr., and her sister, four-year-old Sylvia Mae, moved to 608 South Kent Street in Winchester. Sam left the family for good. Hilda kicked him out.

Patsy would later confide in close friends that Sam had abused her sexually from the time she was eleven. This revelation partly explains Patsy's toughness, her promiscuity, and the succession of lovers and overlapping romances she had throughout her life.

Ginny quit school and went to work at the local drug store as clerk and soda fountain attendant for minimum wage.

"It's more important for us to eat, than for me to get an education,"[5] she said. Hilda, although a fine seamstress, couldn't make enough on her own to support the family. Ginny knew the drugstore job was temporary.

"I'm going to be something one of these days. I won't be doing *this* for the rest of my life." [6]

A customer at the drug store, who heard again and again, Ginny's dream of singing at the Grand Ole Opry, arranged an audition for her and made photographs of her that she could take along in a portfolio. Since there was nowhere to leave the younger children, a neighbor drove Ginny, Hilda, Sam Jr. and Sylvia seven hundred miles, by moonlight, to Nashville. They arrived with time to spare, and took naps on concrete picnic tables in a park. Before the audition, Ginny washed up and changed clothes in the restroom of an Esso gas station.

The Opry audition went well and Ginny was asked to stay an extra day but there was no money for hotel rooms. Besides, Ginny was only sixteen and women had to be eighteen to work for the Opry. That was the rule for both men and women, but for women the rule was enforced.

So they traveled home to Winchester. Ginny found jobs at roadhouses, benefits, barn dances and juke joints, for whatever she could earn to supplement her day job at the drug store. She designed her costumes with detailed sketches, and Hilda sewed them. She dressed in boots and fringe-trimmed cowgirl outfits when she appeared with country bands, and wore cocktail dresses in the nightclubs where she sang ballads and standards.

Hilda had been sixteen when Ginny was born and the two women felt more like sisters together than mother and daughter. Hilda encouraged and assisted Ginny in her quest for a musical stage life. To that end, she introduced Ginny to Jumbo Rinker, a piano player in a supper club in the little town of Martinsburg, West Virginia, just across the state line. On Saturdays, after Ginny worked at the drug store all day, her mother drove her to the club where she sang pop standards with Rinker's small combo. Rinker admired the young songstress, and he and Ginny developed a romantic attachment.

It was through Rinker that Ginny met Bill Peer, a car salesman by day and bandleader by night. When Peer heard Ginny sing in September of 1952, Ginny was twenty years old. He hired her immediately to work with his band. She quit the drug store and performed with Bill Peer and the popular Melody Boys, who played at the Brunswick, Maryland Moose Lodge near Washington D.C. several times a week. Peer encouraged Ginny to take the professional stage name of Patsy, a diminutive of her middle name, Patterson. He mentored her, bought her clothes, promoted her, and tried to get her voice on records. Bill Peer fell in love with his young protégé. But Peer already had a wife.

On March 7, 1953, Patsy married Gerald Cline, who came to the Moose Lodge to hear her sing. Gerald was the secretary for his family's construction business, but didn't report for work very often. He was seven years older than Patsy and had been married and divorced twice. The newlyweds moved first into an apartment in Frederick, Maryland, and then into a trailer home. While Hilda hadn't approved of Patsy's relationship with Peer, a married man, she liked Gerald. But Patsy and Gerald weren't a good match. Patsy yearned for stardom. Gerald wanted a housewife. Patsy found Gerald downright dull, but she took his name and kept it. As Patsy Cline, she became known, regionally, as a singer of country songs.

In 1954, she won first prize singing "Faded Love" at the National Country Music Championships in Warrenton, Virginia, with Bill Peer and the Melody Boys. Later on, she appeared on Billboard charts as "Patsy Kline."

She got the attention of publisher Bill McCall at Four-Star Records. McCall signed on promising singers, controlled their music, paid royalties that were less than par, and made them cover the costs of their recording sessions. Some said he took unfair advantage of the artists. Others defended him, insisting he kept singers and songwriters from starving with advances on their recordings, which he leased to Decca Records or some other big studio. In September of 1954, with Bill Peer and Gerald Cline in attendance, but without a lawyer, Patsy signed a recording contract with McCall.

McCall made a deal with Decca records for Patsy's recordings. She took her first commercial airplane ride to Nashville for her recording session with Owen Bradley, Decca's Nashville representative. Bill Peer was scared to death on the airplane, and held on to the armrests for dear life.

Owen Bradley and his brother, Harold, owned a recording studio called Bradley's Barn. The house that Owen and Harold had converted into the studio wasn't big enough so they added a Quonset hut,* famous for having the best acoustics in Nashville. Harold played guitar. Owen was a first-rate pianist and former bandleader.

Owen Bradley had heard that Patsy was mean and hard to deal with and he dreaded the first meeting. But they got along fine. Peer's band sounded "country," so Owen hired session musicians. A single was released in July of 1955, with her first recording, "A Church, A Courtroom, and Then Goodbye." In January of 1956, in the second session with Bradley, she recorded another single with, "I Love you, Honey," on one side and "Come On In," on the other. The latter song was one Patsy used to open many shows over the years. She felt optimistic about her future.

When Patsy appeared at the Grand Ole Opry for the first time since her underage audition, she thanked Bill Peer for arranging her performance there. It isn't likely that she loved Peer, but he had given Patsy professional and financial support, and many gifts. A fur stole he once gave to her was mailed to Peer's wife by mistake when Patsy left it in a hotel room. Peer's wife sued for divorce, suspecting the affair between Patsy and her husband. When Patsy left Peer's band he was heartbroken.

---

* Quonset hut – a building made of corrugated metal with a semicircular cross section. They were named after Quonset Point, Rhode Island, where the huts were first made during World War Two.

On Friday, April 13, 1956, Patsy met the man she came to love with all her heart–Charlie Dick, a linotype operator at the Winchester Evening Star. Charlie heard her sing with the Kountry Krackers at the Armory in Berryville, Virginia, and fell instantly in love with the lady and her music. A charming guy, Charlie liked to drink and party.

Patsy began singing on the radio with Jimmy Dean of *Town and Country Time,* and by December 1956, she sang with the *Washington DC Jamboree* TV show for a half a million viewers. She wore the western costumes her mother made and developed an audience around DC.

Patsy was not beautiful but she had dramatic features, expressive eyes, creamy skin and a gorgeous figure. She walked with the grace of a dancer and when she entered a room there was an aura about her that gave her center stage. If she liked you, she might call you "Hoss." She loved to kid around with the men backstage over a beer and could tell an off-color joke that would bring a pink shine to some of their faces. Fellow musicians loved her. She saw the stage as an enormous platform–big enough for everybody–and didn't try to out-do her colleagues. She was direct, even blunt, and she liked her friends to match her honesty. She referred to herself as "the Cline." Patsy was a liberated woman before the concept became fashionable.

When Bill McCall told songwriter Don Hecht that he hadn't made any money on Patsy in spite of her powerful voice, Don listened to one of her recordings. Her rich, wonderful sound thrilled him. Around that time, the edges between pop and country were becoming blurred, but he thought she sounded more like a pop singer than a country singer. With Alan Block, Don had written "Walkin' After Midnight," a song he felt was right for Patsy. But Patsy didn't like it.

"It ain't country," she said. She and McCall fought over it, but Hecht brokered a deal. If Patsy could record "A Poor

Man's Roses (or a Rich Man's Gold)"–her song–on the B side, she would sing the ballad for the A side. That's the way Owen Bradley recorded it.

Four-Star Records hadn't yet released "Walkin' After Midnight," when Patsy flew to New York to audition for *The Arthur Godfrey Talent Scouts*, a popular TV show. Janette Davis, the producer of the Godfrey show, listened to Patsy sing country songs, one after the other, and when she heard "Walkin' After Midnight," Davis knew it would be the one to wow the audience. Davis suggested Patsy wear a simple blue dress instead of the cowgirl outfit she brought with her.

On January 21, 1957, Patsy's mother, Hilda, as her "scout," introduced Patsy, who sang for the studio spectators and for a TV audience of about ten million people. An applause meter measured the intensity of the clapping. Patsy won overwhelmingly. As tears rolled down Patsy's cheeks onstage, Hilda cried too, while standing behind the curtain,.

"There's surely stardust on you, Patsy Cline," said Godfrey.[7]

Patsy had renewed her contract with McCall and "Walkin' After Midnight," belonged to him. Released on February 11, the records sold like water in the desert. Patsy received little of the profits, but mail poured into CBS and Decca from people who wanted copies of "Walkin'." Artistic success was hers. She presented a new publicity photo of herself to her mother and signed it, "We finally made it. Patsy."

On February 16, she sang "Walkin After Midnight," for the audience at the Grand Ole Opry. Patsy wept for joy at the roaring applause.

Bob Crosby, a bandleader and emcee on radio and TV, with a voice as sweet as his brother Bing's, invited Patsy to his West coast show. He paid her the highest fee she had ever earned, $1500.00 for three performances.

Patsy's father, Sam Hensley died in 1957. When they heard he was ill, Patsy and Hilda visited him in the hospital where he lay on his deathbed. During the weeks after his death, Patsy sang

"Railway to Heaven," and other songs she'd sung with her dad when she was a child and tried to forgive him. Hilda apparently did forgive him. She reserved a burial plot for herself next to Sam's at the National Cemetery in Winchester.

Gerald Cline filed for divorce in January after the couple had been separated for some time. Patsy lived at her mother's and then in a rented mobile home. When the divorce became final in March of 1957, Patsy and Charlie Dick wanted to marry, but Charlie was drafted into the Army and left for boot camp at Fort Benning.

Patsy and Charlie celebrated her 25th birthday on September 8, at the Moose Lodge. Bill Peer's band was on stage and the audience called for Patsy to sing. Patsy didn't really want to go on stage, and Peer, who had moved on with his life, seemed neutral about the prospect as well, but she couldn't deny her fans. She performed one last time with Peer.

On September 15, 1957, Patsy and Charlie were married in Winchester at Hilda's house on Kent Street in a joyous celebration. They moved to Fayetteville, NC, near Fort Bragg where Charlie was stationed. Patsy traveled for singing gigs and commuted to Nashville to make records over the next few months. She was stuck with McCall's mediocre songs and Decca didn't promote her records because McCall didn't include funds for advertising and promotion into his payments to Decca.

In 1957, at the Dee Jay convention, Patsy received Billboard's "Most Promising Country and Western Female Artist" award. Music Vendor magazine also awarded her with "Greatest Achievement in Records" for "Walkin' After Midnight."

Patsy's first child Julie Simadore, was born in Winchester on August 25, 1958. Patsy had come home to have Hilda close by and stayed there with the baby for a while. She felt pleased to have a daughter, "my own piece of me," [8] but before long she felt restless and missed the singing life.

When Charlie was discharged from the Army in February of 1959, he held odd jobs in Winchester, but money was in short supply. The couple wanted to be near the Opry and other work possibilities. In August of 1959, the Dicks moved to Nashville and rented a house in Madison, on 213 Marthona Drive off of Hickory Boulevard. Pearl and Carl Butler, friends from the Opry, welcomed them heartily to Nashville, and soon Patsy and Charlie made many other close friends.

Charlie found a job as a linotype operator at the Curley Printing Company with a salary of $110 per week, and Patsy went on tour, singing with Faron Young* making $25 and later $50 a night. Her traveling expenses were paid and the salary was considered good for a woman of that era. Working with Faron, a country star with a mellow, tenor voice, she continued to develop her style.

In January of 1960, Patsy became a member of the Grand Ole Opry, a lifelong dream fulfilled. At $25 a night–take home pay was fifteen to twenty dollars–she earned less than the male performers but she tolerated the wage inequity just as other women did during the mid-twentieth century in America.

The first Opry broadcasts aired live from the WSM studio in 1925 and the response was so tremendous that it moved twice to larger theaters before WSM bought the Ryman Auditorium in Nashville in the mid-1940s. The Ryman would be the Opry's home for 31 years. Bluegrass, folk, country, Western and gospel music found its most enthusiastic audiences there. The entire country talked about the "Nashville Sound," which was said to have originated with Elvis Presley's "Don't Be Cruel." "The sound" evolved and changed. Strings replaced fiddles and choruses sang backup to the singers. Another element of "the sound," was the effect of musicians playing

---

* Faron Young and Patsy had met on a Connie Gay show in Washington DC. They worked together often over the years.

together and recording live what hadn't yet been written on a sheet of music. Once, Patsy refused quite a profitable gig to stay in Nashville and sing at the Ryman. On a bio for the Opry's WSM radio studio, she said, "I don't want to be rich, just live good." [9]

The Ryman wasn't air-conditioned in those days. After the shows, the performers dashed across the alley behind the theatre and flocked into Tootsies, which was cooled. On red and white tablecloths, they drank cold beer, ate delicious hamburgers, told jokes and celebrated life. Opry members didn't earn much and Tootsie allowed the country stars to run a tab.

Patsy liked a sexy look on stage. For her nightclub work she wore tight fitting clothes, ruby red lipstick and dangling earrings. She appeared for work one evening in gold lamé trousers, not the down-home look the Opry aspired to. Not only was the outfit too risqué, she had broken the unwritten rule that only the men wore pants at the Opry. Officials made her change clothes.

Patsy had a magnificent voice, which reached the back of a large hall without a microphone. She could have sung operetta had she wanted to. Her pitch was true and perfect and her diction crisp and clean, though one might notice a bit of a Virginia twang at times. She could learn a melody after hearing it once.

Owen Bradley believed in Patsy and helped her to record new songs from Four-Star, a shade better than the usual offerings. He backed her up with a male quartet, the Jordanaires,* who also sang with Elvis Presley.** At first she resisted with her usual contrariness.

---

* The Jordanaires – a back-up and gospel singing quartet, the original group consisting of Gordon Stoker, Hoyt Hawkins, Neal Matthews, Jr., and Ray Walker. They sang on all but one of Patsy's 20 recording sessions from 1959 to 1963.

"...I don't want no four male voices covering me up," [8] she said, embarrassing the men. Owen took her aside for a little talk before she relented and approved the plan. Over time, Patsy came to love the Jordanaires, who sang the background vocals for many of her future songs.

In January of 1959, Bradley recorded Patsy singing two gospel songs, backed by the Jordanaires, "Just a Closer Walk With Thee, and "Life's Railway to Heaven." Four-Star had nothing to offer, and since Patsy needed to work, they chose songs from the public domain in an attempt to get her out of the rut she'd been in since her success with "Walkin' After Midnight."

Patsy still wasn't sure of her style. Bradley encouraged blues and torch songs because she cried as she sang them and you could hear the tears in her voice.

Her marriage was stormy. Sometimes she came to the recording studio with tears in her eyes.

"Me and Charlie had a row."[10] Charlie Dick drank too much and had flings and affairs. Patsy, too, had romantic trysts on the road. Charlie and Patsy were madly in love one day and cursing one another the next. "That's the way we were. Both of us stubborn," said Charlie in a telephone interview with this author, "but we had good times too."

Patsy was always strapped for cash, and in order to earn advances she had renewed with McCall twice over the years and was tied to him and to his lackluster material, until the fall of 1960. She wanted a manager to help her out of the contract

---

** Patsy loved Elvis, whose rise to fame brought a new style to country music. A picture of Elvis adorned a scrapbook Patsy gave to her friend, Dottie West, shortly before the fatal plane crash. In addition to the Opry stars and Elvis, Patsy admired Jo Stafford, Patti Page and Helen Morgan.

and to sign her with Decca Records. She wanted some decent songs to record.

Ramsey (Randy) Hughes had played guitar with the Opry since age fifteen.   He also managed Lloyd "Cowboy" Copas, bringing the country music singer back to stardom from a slump. Randy played guitar for Cowboy Copas and fell in love with and married his daughter, Kathy Copas, a singer who performed with her father. Kathy gave up singing when she and Randy expected their first child. Retiring from singing to be wife and mother was the order of the day for pregnant performers at the Opry, unlike Patsy who wanted both career and motherhood.

The first time Randy heard Patsy sing, he told Kathy that he had just heard "the best voice the world has ever known." Patsy liked Randy. Owen Bradley and Charlie agreed that Randy was honest and good at his work, and that Patsy needed a manager.

Randy took charge of Patsy's career, booked her gigs and accompanied her to performance destinations. He allowed the complicated contract with McCall to continue until it ran out. Then Owen Bradley gave Patsy a $1000 fee and signed her with Decca Records for three years with an option to renew.* Finally, she could select from a list of good songs and Decca had the budget to promote her records.

Meanwhile, Randy and Patsy were on the road together and Randy became Patsy's anchor and caretaker. At home in Nashville, Patsy and Charlie fought. If the fights got out of hand, Patsy called the police or she awakened Randy by phone call in the night to come and rescue her from an irate husband.

---

* She had an offer from RCA, but she felt comfortable with Bradley and wanted to continue working with him.

She sang at the Opry on January 21, and came home for a restless night's sleep. The next day, a son, Allen Randolph was born. Charlie had been out partying late into the night and when Patsy needed to go to the hospital early that morning, a neighbor drove her because she couldn't waken Charlie.

Bradley wanted Patsy to record "I Fall to Pieces." She didn't like the song. Regardless of her protests, Bradley insisted. Patsy was allowed to record "Faded Love," on the B-side if she would sing "I Fall to Pieces," for the A-side. She went on to sing "I Fall to Pieces," at all of her road shows and sock hops over the next weeks and the Dee Jays broadcast it all over the country. It rose slowly on the charts and stayed near the top for 39 weeks, then descended slowly. Finally, Patsy had a hit and the money she earned was hers–and Randy's, of course–to keep. With her first royalty check she bought new appliances for Hilda's kitchen. Patsy had already helped her mother buy a better house down the way, on Kent Street.

On a Delta Airlines flight from California, on April 22, 1961, Patsy had a premonition that she would be in a car wreck. She wrote out a will on Delta stationary and had it witnessed,[*] though it wasn't legally filed.

Patsy invited her mother Hilda, her brother Sam Jr. and her sister Sylvia, to Nashville to celebrate Sylvia's graduation from high school. She planned to take them all to the Opry. On Wednesday, June 14, 1961, she and Sam, who was driving, motored home from a shopping trip and were hit head-on by a

---

[*] In the will, she provided for the children's education. She expressed her wishes regarding the disposition of her possessions. She stipulated that Hilda should raise the children, and that if Hilda passed away, her sister, Sylvia should take them. She gave instructions that she be dressed in a Western outfit of her own design, buried at the place of her husband's choosing with her wedding ring on, and with certain tokens from her children at her side in the casket.

"woman driver" coming from the opposite direction, trying to pass another car on a hill. Patsy went through the windshield and almost died from loss of blood. Lying in the grass at the scene, she insisted the other victims be taken to the hospital first. One passenger in the other vehicle was killed. Sam had chest injuries and Patsy broke her wrist, dislocated her hip and received severe lacerations to her face. Sam recovered in the hospital after two weeks but Patsy spent the next two months there recuperating from her injuries.

She was in critical condition over the first two days. The switchboard took constant calls from fans and friends. Cards and letters arrived from all over the country and flowers covered her room. During her hospital stay, "I Fall to Pieces," made number one on the country charts.

"It took 10 nurses to tie me to the bed," [11] said Patsy to her first audience when she finally went back to work. She felt humbled and grateful by the success. At the same time she had always known she would make it.

"Damn, it's about time. I've paid my dues,"[12] she told her friend, Dottie West.

She needed more time to heal. She could barely walk with her crutches when she was discharged from the hospital. Headaches plagued her for months. Severe scars resulted from the wounds on her forehead. She wore heavy makeup and arranged her hair to conceal them. Sometimes she wore wigs.

Charlie quit his job to care for the children, to help Patsy get around, and to accompany her on tour. For a while their relationship improved. Patsy, glad to be alive after her accident, wanted to live a better life and to have a better marriage.

Determined to resume her road tours, she traveled to Tulsa to sing with the Cimarron Boys at their own theatre. She sat on a stool near the mike, her crutches by her side. It was July 29, 1961, and her first engagement since her accident. She had to pace herself. She began with, "Come On In (and sit right down and make yourself at home,)" her signature opener. Then she sang every song she knew and complimented the band graciously and repeatedly. Much of the performance was recorded. You can hear her today on the CD, *Patsy Cline, Live From the Cimarron Ballroom,* and listen to her laughing and joking with the audience and musicians, and enjoy the versatility and power of her singing.

"I'm having the time of my life,"[13] she told the crowd. To the band, she said, "Put it in a gear of about a B-flat, and kick it off, boys," and she would carry the beat, never getting behind.

August of 1961 found her returning to Bradley's Barn, though her ribs still hurt. She recorded "San Antonio Rose," "The Wayward Wind," and "Seven Lonely Days," among others, for an album, *Patsy Cline's Showcase.* She sang beautifully but she wasn't satisfied with the track for "Crazy," one of the selections for the album. She came back in October to dub in the vocals for "Crazy." She joked, "I just hope I don't try to live up to this 'Crazy' bit, like I did the last one."[14] (referring to her car wreck after "I Fall to Pieces.")

Randy booked Patsy in Las Vegas for $6800 per week at The Merry Mint, an off the strip casino/theater with a small stage and tight dressing rooms. TomPall and the Glaser Brothers sang back up, and once the Glaser Brothers and the musicians had been paid, and other expenses had been covered, the Dicks cleared $2000 a week to send home to the bank in Nashville.

Patsy sang four 45-minute sold-out shows every night for five weeks and got the "Vegas throat," a condition in which the vocal cords develop ulcers due to dry air, and probably overwork. For some performances, she had to lip-sync over her records played back stage. Her gig extended through the Christmas holidays and Patsy flew her family out for a visit. Even with her family there, she wanted to be home. She cried on stage, felt blue, and didn't really like Las Vegas. She insisted she would never return, just as Randy negotiated better wages for her next engagement there.

Don Hecht came to Vegas to see her perform. Patsy told him that the song he had written, and that she had recorded, "Cry Not for Me," represented her own thoughts about how folks should think of her after she'd gone.

When she and Charlie purchased her dream house in Nashville, a $30,000 red brick structure on Nella Drive, she called it "the house that Vegas built." Once, while viewing a film, she had watched "some rich dame" lolling in a luxurious bubble bath surrounded by walls that were speckled with gold. Patsy found golden flecks dotting the white tiles surrounding a sink in one of the bathrooms of the new house, a little gold dust of their own. The children, Julie and Randy, each had a bedroom. The recreation room became the music center where she and Charlie decorated the walls with album covers. Patsy shopped for the perfect furnishings for her parlor, including a sofa covered in light green silk.

With her own house completed, Patsy announced that she wouldn't be happy until she could build her mother one just like it.

Patsy revered the writers who composed her songs. She hung out with them at Tootsies and invited them to her house. Because they knew her so well, their songs echoed Patsy's life and she sang them with tear jerking pathos. "That's How a Heartache Begins," by Harlan Howard,* and "Why Can't He Be You," by Hank Cochran, were songs written by friends who knew her struggle.

---

* Harland Howard, from California, had earned large royalties from "Heartaches by the Number," which had hit the country and pop charts. He bought himself a new Cadillac and moved to Nashville. His wife Jan Harland, sang at the Grand Ole Opry. It was Jan's demonstration recording of the Howard/Cochran tune, "I Fall to Pieces," that drew Bradley's interest in the song for Patsy.

Hank Cochran called Patsy at home in December of 1961 and said he'd written the perfect song for her. On and on he praised the brilliance of the piece.

"...Come on over and let's hear the...masterpiece,"[15] said Patsy and told Hank that if he wanted a drink, to stop by the liquor store and pick up a bottle. Patsy and Charlie didn't usually keep a supply of liquor at home. Hank arrived and performed his creation, "She's Got You." Patsy loved the song. She and Hank shared a few drinks while she listened and learned the lyrics. Patsy sang it over the phone for Randy, who adored it. She recorded it on December 17, with immediate success. "She's Got You," was the first of her hits that she had chosen herself and that she and Owen Bradley both liked.

She had not taken many vacations. In the early years of her career, she was on the road for weeks at the time to earn the meager wages necessary to keep the family going. After her success, she toured constantly to satisfy the demands of her fans. But now, exhausted, and still suffering the headaches and emotional pain resulting from the car crash, Patsy took two weeks off to rest.

Performers often took to the road in Cadillacs, five to a car, and covered long distances, as much as 500 miles, and sometimes rode all night to make show times. Patsy once said, "If you want to know what country music is all about I'll tell you. It's singing in clubs and sleazy joints, traveling on dusty, rutted roads, and staying in motels that have seen better days. It's signing autographs and posing for pictures and doing the best job you can. It's meaning something special to a whole bunch of strangers who you'll probably never see again but suddenly become like family."[16]

As "Crazy" and "She's Got You" hit the big time, and the money rolled in, Randy got his pilot's license and bought a green and white Piper Comanche. He could shorten commuting times by flying them to their tour destinations. But he was licensed to fly only under Visual Flight Rules and did not have an instrument rating.

Randy demanded higher fees for her appearances and she no longer worked roadhouses and taverns.

"I'm slowin' down,"[17] said Patsy.

"Now's the time to work," said Randy.

"We're rakin' it in all right, but there ain't a minute to spend it," said Patsy. "I'm working more than I should and feeling the worse for it. And I hate going out on the road four and five days a week and leaving behind my babies." [17]

Hilda Hensley continued to sew Patsy's costumes. Onto one of the Las Vegas gowns, Hilda had sewn hundreds of sequins by hand. She made shirtwaist dresses in all colors and patterns. They fit Patsy to perfection and she wore them elegantly. During the time when Jackie Kennedy donned her simple, classic clothes, Patsy joined countless women the world over who took style cues from Camelot's first lady.

When Patsy sang with the Opry at Carnegie Hall,* Hilda traveled to New York for the event. And when Patsy sang with Johnny Cash's troupe at the Hollywood Bowl,** Hilda sat in the audience.

Patsy had always been generous. As her financial situation improved she gave her friends and protégés clothes, costumes and money to pay the rent. Dottie West, Loretta Lynn, Brenda Lee, Barbara Mandrell and Pearl Butler are all witnesses to her magnanimous nature. On road trips she watched over the

---

* The Opry came to Carnegie Hall to sing a benefit for the Music Aid Society from which the earnings provided assistance to retired opera staff and stars. When Dorothy Kilgallen, journalist and TV panelist, referred to the Opry stars as the Carnegie Hillbillies, Patsy retaliated and called Kilgallen "the wicked witch of the East."

** The tour with Johnnie Cash, "Shower of Stars," went on to Phoenix, Tucson, El Paso and Albuquerque.

younger female singers with protective friendship. She also gave advice. "If you can't do it with feeling, don't do it." And she believed in putting a fine finish on a song–a lyrical flourish, a line to remember. "Let's take it home," she sometimes called out on stage, toward the end of a rousing melody. Her style was widely emulated. Patsy tore through the established model, and changed forever the perception of what a female country singer should look like and what the subjects of her songs should be.

She took several tours with Johnny Cash and his band *The Tennessee Three*, taking second billing only to Cash. Johnny Western* opened the show and introduced performers such as June Carter, Barbara Mandrell, George Jones, and Gordon Terry. Patsy would usually appear after the intermission. Cash appeared last, after Patsy. Sometimes the tours would be one-nighters and sometimes ten days long. Charlie stayed at home.

After a West-coast Television appearance, Patsy and June Carter hit the road to do a couple of two-woman shows in California nightclubs. Patsy sang and June told jokes or they sang together when they both knew the songs. Leaving Oxnard, Patsy told June she wanted to drive the car so that June could listen and write.

"I want you to write all this down, because I'm going out soon, and I'm really going out fast, and it's going to be tragic."[18] June wrote the instructions on a pad in the dark of the car, with a cigarette lighter to illuminate the page. Patsy told June she wanted her mother to raise Julie and Charlie to raise Randy. "I want them to bring my body home to my house." [19]

---

*Johnny Western became famous for co-writing the "Ballad of Paladin," the closing theme song of the TV program, *Have Gun, Will Travel*, and performing the song.

Patsy's premonitions led her to believe that she would never reach her thirtieth birthday. However, she did celebrate her thirtieth by throwing a party in her "dream house" in Nashville. Guests included Loretta and Doolittle Lynn, Dottie and Bill West, Jan and Harlan Howard, Randy and Kathy Hughes, the Cochran's, Faron Young, Minnie Pearl and many others.

Patsy had several satisfying recording sessions with Owen Bradley. They recorded a number of standards in the legendary Quonset hut, including this author's personal favorites, "True Love," by Cole Porter, and "Always," by Irving Berlin.

"You know," said Irving Berlin, "I don't even like country music but there is no one who sings my song "Always," like Patsy Cline."

In all she recorded 102 songs, precisely half of them for Four-Star and half for Decca Records.

During the first of four recording evenings in February of 1963, Patsy sang a number of oldies, including, "Faded Love," Someday You'll want Me to Want You," and Love Letters in the Sand." The musicians included Floyd Cramer on piano, Harold Bradley, electric bass, Bob Moore on standup bass, Grady Martin, electric guitar, Randy Hughes, Guitar, and Buddy Harmon on drums, along with ten violinists. From the control room during one session, Bradley saw Charlie enter the studio and told him to leave.

"What did I do? I just got here,"[20] said Charlie.

"She's cried on every song she's done. I don't want to break the mood. I don't want her to see you, so get out of here."[21] Charlie walked back through the door.

Randy flew Patsy, Charlie and himself to Birmingham for a singing gig. By the time they reached Birmingham, Patsy had a cold and didn't feel well, but she performed anyway to an adoring audience.

She had committed to doing a benefit concert in Kansas City for the wife and children of Jack Wesley Call, "Cactus Jack," a disc jockey who had been killed in an automobile accident. "Count me in..."[22] she had said when they asked her if she would join the large group of country stars who would donate their time and talents. After four hours sleep, Randy, Patsy and Charlie flew from Birmingham to Nashville to let Charlie off the plane and to pick up fellow performers Hawkshaw Hawkins* and Cowboy Copas. They flew on to Kansas City.

Attendees can't seem to remember if there were two shows or three. Patsy was the headliner for the concerts, appearing along with Hawkins, Cowboy, Randy, Dottie West and a large cast. Although trying to shake the flu, Patsy wore a stunning white gown, gave grand performances, sang all her hits, and thanked the audience as if they were the stars. "I love you, all," [23] she told them, tears in her eyes. The benefit raised $3000.

Bad weather descended on Kansas City and on the morning after the concert the airport was closed. Patsy, burning "to get home to my babies," briefly considered riding with Dottie and Bill West who had made the 16-hour trip to Kansas City from Nashville by car. But after she had packed her bags, when she saw Dottie in the lobby of the hotel where they'd all spent the night, Patsy told her she'd decided to fly with Randy. She thought the airport would open soon and that she and Randy would get home sooner than would the car travelers. Dottie expressed concern about Patsy flying through the wretched weather, but Patsy blew it off.

"Hoss, don't worry about me 'cause when it comes my time to go, I'm going."[24] Patsy, Randy, Hawkshaw and Cowboy

---

* Hawkshaw Hawkins was an American country singer and songwriter, a member of the Grand Ole Opry, married to Jean Shepard, also a country star. Hawkins and Jean were expecting their second child when Hawkins was killed in the ill-fated Piper Comanche.

ended up spending another night in Kansas City while the airport was closed.

Patsy called her mother early Tuesday to say the fog had cleared but there were thunderstorms everywhere. Four passengers finally took off from Kansas City at 1:30, crammed into the tiny aircraft, Hawkins up front with Randy, so he could stretch his tall self out, and Patsy and Copas in the rear. It was March 5, 1963. They crossed Missouri and Arkansas, landing at times to allow the storms and weather to get ahead of them. They made a fuelling stop in Dyersburg, Tenn. It was raining when they left Dyersburg but Randy's wife had told him by phone, on the ground in Dyersburg, that it had stopped raining in Nashville, their destination. Severe turbulence was forecast. The station manager cautioned them against flight but they departed anyway at 6:07.

When the wreck was found in the hills of Tennessee, the clock on the dashboard of what remained of the shattered aircraft read 6:20. The pilot, Randy Hughes was thirty-five, Cowboy Copas,* forty-nine, Hawkshaw Hawkins, forty-one, and Patsy, thirty. Their bodies had been torn asunder in the crash.

"In 1964 the Civil Aeronautics Board claimed the probable cause of the crash was a 'Non-instrument pilot attempting visual flight in adverse weather conditions, resulting in a loss of control. Judgment of the pilot in initiating flight in the existing conditions was misguided.'"[25]

In life, Patsy said, "I've played hard, but I've worked hard." As if life were a race to the finish, she had plowed through it with fierce determination.

At the Country Music Festival in Nashville in 1962, in the ballroom of the Andrew Jackson Hotel, she'd worn a gold

---

* Kathy Copas Hughes lost both her husband and her father in the crash.

brocade gown and gold spiked heels.   Never one to hide her exhilaration, she added a tiara, her own emblem of success. That year, *Billboard* named her "Favorite Female Artist." *Cashbox* titled her with "Most Programmed Country and Western Female," and "Most Programmed Album of the Year."   She won "Female Vocalist of the Year" awards from *Music Vendor* and from *Music Reporter* for "Crazy," and "She's Got You." *Music Reporter* named Patsy, "Star of the Year."

Patsy had her first British hit with "She's Got You," and there had been talk, before her death, of a European tour.   She expected to have some plastic surgery for the scars on her face and some cosmetic work on her teeth, which were chipped.

She didn't get to those things or to experience her Grammy or the stardom that magnified posthumously.   *The Patsy Cline Story*, an album of songs that Owen Bradley released shortly after her death became an unqualified all-time hit.   Song-play tributes, such as *Always...Patsy Cline*, celebrating her life, flowed into theater world.   A movie, *Sweet Dreams,* named after one of her hit songs, featured Jessica Lange as Patsy.

In 1973, Patsy was inducted posthumously into the *The Country Music Hall of Fame,* the first solo female performer ever to hold that title.   Johnny Cash announced the award.   Since August 3, 1999, Patsy has a star on the Hollywood Walk of Fame, unveiled by Charlie Dick and his daughter, Julie. Patsy's music is competitive in today's market nearly half a century after her death.

Her prediction came true that she would, one day, come to Winchester and draw "one hell of a crowd."   Twenty-five thousand people lined the streets for her funeral.

Patsy's Gravestone at the Shenandoah Memorial Park in Winchester, Virginia. The inscription reads "Death Cannot Kill What Never Dies."

Next Page: The Patsy Cline Historic House. The Hensley's former home at 608 Kent Street in Winchester is now a lovely museum to Patsy, complete with guides and gift shop.   Photo by Jerald Watts

07/27/2013

66

Patsy Cline
Bibliography:

Bego, Mark, *I Fall to Pieces: The Music and the Life of Patsy Cline* Adams Media Corp. Holbrook, MA: 1995

Brown, Stuart E. Jr. and Myers, Lorraine F. *Patsy Cline: Singing Girl from the Shenandoah Valley* Virginia Book Company, Berryville, Virginia: 1996

Gomery, Douglas, *Patsy Cline: The Making of an Icon*, Trafford Publishing: 2011

Hazen, Cindy & Freeman, Mike *Love Always, Patsy: Patsy Cline's Letters to a Friend* Berkley Publishing Group, New York, NY: 1999

Hofstra, Warren R., Editor, *Sweet Dreams The World of Patsy Cline* University of Illinois Press, Urbana, Chicago and Springfield: 2013

Jones, Margaret *Patsy: The Life and Times of Patsy Cline* Da Capo Press, New York, NY: 1999

Kingsbury, Paul *The Grand Ole Opry History of Country Music: 70 years of the songs, the stars, and the stories.* Villard Books of Random House, New York and Canada: 1995

Lynn, Loretta with Vecsey, George, *Loretta Lynn: Coal Miner's Daughter* Da Capo Press, New York, NY: 1976

Nassour, Ellis, *Honky Tonk Angel: The Intimate Story of Patsy Cline* Chicago Review Press, Chicago, Ill: 2008

Nassour, Ellis, *Patsy Cline: An Intimate Biography* Tower Publications, Inc. New York NY: 1981

Quotes:

1. "Oh no, Patsy…" Page 191 Nassour, Ellis, 2008
2. "Owen Bradley and Patsy Cline…" Page 211 Gomery, Douglas 2011
3. "a voice that boomed…" Page 9 Brown and Myers
4. "One of these days…" Page XII Intro, Jones, Margaret
5. "It's more important…" Page 17 Brown and Myers

6.   "I'm going to be..." Page 20 Jones, Margaret

7.   "There's surely stardust...Page 75 Nassour, Ellis, 2008

8.   "...my own piece of me." Page 163 Jones, Margaret

9.   " I don't want..." Page 168 Jones, Margaret

10. "Me and Charlie..." Page 103 Nassour, Ellis, 2008

11. *"It took ten nurses..."* The CD *Patsy Cline, Live at the Cimarron Theatre*

12. " Damn, It's about time..." Page X Forward by Dottie West, Nassour, Ellis, 2008

13. *"I'm havin' the time..."* The CD, *Patsy Cline, Live at the Cimarron Theatre*

14. "I just hope..." Page 234 Jones, Margaret

15. "Cut the B.S...." Page 235 Jones, Margaret

16. "If you want to..." Page 105 Nassour, Ellis, 2008

17. "I'm slowin' down." Page 197 Nassour, Ellis, 2008

18. "I want you to write..." Page 181 Bego, Mark

19. "I want them to bring..." Page 181 Bego, Mark

20. "What did I do?..." Page 213 Nassour, Ellis, 2008

21. "She's cried on every..." Page 213 Nassour, 2008

22. "Count me in..." Page 284 Jones, Margaret

23. "I love you all..."Page 286 Jones, Margaret

24. "Hoss, don't worry..." Page 223 Nassour, Ellis, 2008

25. "In 1964, the Civil Aeronautic..." Page 247 Nassour

More Notes – Patsy Cline

Page 41 - "Like the young Virginia" (growing up poor) Page 211, *Patsy Cline The Making of an Icon*, Donald Gomery, hereafter referred to as Gomery
Page 42 - Each week bands came...Page 49 - Gomery

Temple Glen – Page 5 - *Honky Tonk Angel The Intimate Story of Patsy Cline*, Ellis Nassour, 2008, hereafter referred to as Nassour

"The Old Rugged Cross" – Page 16 – *Singing Girl from the Shenandoah Valley*, Stuart E. Brown, Jr. and Lorraine F. Myers, hereafter referred to as Brown and Myers

Stable home life at Washington and Lee – Page 44 – Gomery

Living next to the Shenandoah River, Hilda's fishing and gardening Page 39 – Gomery

Footnote – Sam's other children – Page 4 – *Patsy The Life and Times of Patsy Cline*, Margaret Jones, hereafter referred to as M. Jones
Page 43 - Classmates saw her as "pushy." Page 9 – Brown and Myers
Patsy would later confide – Page 10 – M. Jones
Page 45 - The newlyweds moved – Page 37 – Brown and Myers
"Patsy Kline" – Page 40 – Brown and Myers
Page 46 - Bill was terrified of flying – Page 36 – Nassour
Page 47 - She's not a country singer. – Page 63 – Nassour
Page 48 - Simple blue dress – Page 130 – M. Jones
Bob Crosby – Page 141 – M. Jones
Page 51 - Checkered tablecloths Page 148 – *I Fall to Pieces, The music and life of Patsy Cline* - Mark Bego, hereafter referred to as Bego
Tootsie allowed the opry singers to run tabs. Page 134 – Bego
Page 51 - Patsy's voice – Forward by Dottie West – Nassour
Page 54 - Footnote – summary of the will – Page 133 – Bego
Page 56 - Don Hecht and "Cry Not For Me" – Page 179 – Bego
"some rich dame" and the gold wallpaper – Page 261 M. Jones
Page 57 - Footnote – Harland Howard – Page 196 – M. Jones
Jan's demonstration recording – 201 M. Jones
Page 59 - Footnote – Opry and Carnegie Hall, Dorothy Kilgallen and "the wicked witch of the East" - Page 175 and 176 – Nassour
Page 61 - "You know, Irving Berlin said…" – Page 206 – Gomery
she recorded 102 songs – Page 184 – Bego
Page 64 - As many as 25,000 people – Page 93 – Brown and Myers
Charlie Dick and Julie unveiled Patsy's star – Page 25 – Gomery

Discography:

Best of Patsy Cline Curb Records, Burbank, CA: 1991
Patsy Cline: Live At The Cimarron Ballroom MCA Records Nashville: 1997
Patsy Cline: Pick Me Up On Your Way Down BRISA U.K.: 1995
The Patsy Cline Story MCA Records, Universal City, California: 1973, 1988
Patsy Cline: Sweet Dreams The Complete Decca Studio Masters 1960 to 1063, Geffen Records Santa Monica, CA: 2010

Videography:

Opry Video Classics Hall-of-Fame Time/Life DVD/Video, Grand Ole Ory, Gaylord Entertainment Company, 2007

Cass Elliot 1973, (Bettmann/Corbis Images)

Cass Elliot   (1941 – 1974)

Ellen Naomi Cohen was born in Baltimore, Maryland on September 18, 1941, the first child of Bess and Philip Cohen. Philip adored opera. Bess loved show tunes and jazz and had briefly sung with the renowned *Fred Waring Orchestra*. Ellen grew up in a musical atmosphere, and from an early age she could carry her own in a three-part harmony. By the time she started school, she sang, gave recitations and blossomed from the attention of an audience.

A sister Leah, was born in 1948 and a brother Joseph, three years later. Joseph and Leah also took musical paths but it was Ellen, as Cass Elliot, who became a star.

As a child, she accompanied her father to a stage performance of the opera, *La Boheme*. In the last act, as the dying Mimi struggled for breath, Ellen called out from the audience, "Won't somebody please get a doctor? She's really sick." [1] All of her life Ellen's sense of reality would be cloaked in dreams and drama.

During her youth, the Cohens moved between Baltimore, Alexandria, and the suburbs of Washington D.C. while her father worked to develop a successful catering business. After World War II, money was scarce, and both parents took jobs to meet the expenses of their growing family.

When Leah was expected, Ellen was seven years old with a contagious skin condition. To protect the new baby, Ellen lived for some weeks with her grandparents, who encouraged her to eat. She gained weight around that time.

"I've been fat since I was seven," [2] said Ellen later in life, after she'd changed her name to Cass Elliot. Every time she switched schools, other kids mocked her and made crude remarks. She pretended to ignore them but suffered silently.

Concerned about the extra pounds, Ellen's parents sent her to a psychologist but she didn't benefit from the sessions. Reality for Ellen came from her imagination. When the truth hurt it was natural to mask it through fantasy. Bess and Philip supervised Ellen's taking of amphetamines to reduce her appetite but the pills made her feel jittery and she stopped taking them. So weight issues continued to plague her.

At age 15, a move to Baltimore required another change of schools. In the fashion-conscious Forest Park High School, the right clothes were expected, and by comparison Ellen wore bizarre looking outfits, sometimes covering her bitten-off nails with white gloves. She worked in her father's mobile food stand for several hours before school, and looked tired and disheveled by the time she arrived in class. Fortunately, Ellen loved to cut up and crack jokes and won many friends with her wit and charm. For all her jocular facade, however, an inner ache haunted her.

At Forest Park High, Sharon Lisenbee, who became a life-long friend, insisted that Ellen be invited into her sorority. Both young women majored in music and sang in the choir. After school they sat in Sharon's basement listening to Broadway musicals. On Saturday nights they often went to the movies together.

During the summer before her senior year of high school, the Hilltop Theatre of Owing Mills held auditions. Ellen urged Sharon to try out and she drove the two of them to the theatre ten miles out of town in her Dad's old car. Sharon could sing and dance and she won parts in *Bells are Ringing* and *The Boyfriend*. Ellen hung around the theatre that summer learning all the speaking parts in the plays and making friends with cast members. When the French maid role became available in *The Boyfriend*, she got the part. She sang, "It's nicer, much nicer, in Nice." For the next play, *Prior to Broadway*, she walked silently onto the stage, dressed as a clown, to post a placard on an easel announcing the next scene.

This taste of theatre life gave Ellen an appetite for more. She quit school a few months before graduation, attending night school to earn the half credit needed to enter college. Then she begged her parents to give her five years to try to make it on Broadway. With their consent she struck out on her own for Manhattan.*

Ellen had fun throughout her life with language riddles and backward spellings. She wanted a new name to go along with her new life in New York. Since her father had already nicknamed her Cass and she was used to answering to that moniker, she took the C from Cohen to make Cass, the E from Ellen to make Elliot, reversing her former initials.

As Cass Elliot she drove to New York City, the American hub of theatre and music, and moved in with her Aunt Lil. Not understanding the risks of the inner city, she left her car unlocked while unpacking, returning to find it empty, her favorite clothes and possessions gone–a bitter beginning. But soon she got a job as a hatcheck girl and began going to auditions.

She made the tryout finals, but the part of Miss Marmelstein in *I Can Get it for You Wholesale* went to another up and coming singer, Barbra Streisand. Cass did get a small part in a touring production of *The Music Man.*

In 1961, while she was traveling with the show, her father was involved in a car accident. Sadly, he died a week later of his injuries at the age of forty-two. Many friends attended Philip's funeral, a testament to his good-natured generosity.

Philip had always wanted to own a Cadillac. In the limo behind the hearse, on the way to the funeral, Cass said to her younger siblings, "Well, at least Dad finally got to ride in a brand new frigging Cadillac." [3] After laughing, they worried about making jokes on such a solemn occasion, but then

---

* Some said that she hated "the buses"–her father's mobile diners–and that she escaped to avoid working them.

decided, "Daddy would want us to." Cass loved her father and mourned his death.

She moved into the basement apartment of her mother's house in Alexandria to help care for her younger siblings, Leah and Joseph, and enrolled at the American University in the District of Columbia as a speech and drama student. For a few weeks, Cass became involved in the campus radio station.

Steeped in music and music history, Cass offered entertaining repartee on the jazz program she announced. She knew the words to the popular songs of the day, and while playing records for the listening audience, Cass crooned along with Ella Fitzgerald and Billie Holiday. Colleagues noticed her beautiful voice. Alan Pollock, the producer, became her first boyfriend. Both were Jewish, from Baltimore, and loved jazz. Alan remained a life-long friend.

Always, Cass's bent had been toward ballads, show tunes, drama and theatre, but folk music had caught on with the college crowd; Woody Guthrie, Pete Seeger, Joan Baez and The Kingston Trio owned the airwaves. Cass developed a sense of what listeners wanted to hear.

In 1963 she met Tim Rose, "a man with a banjo." Awed by Cass's voice and her perfect pitch, Tim wanted to sing with her. He convinced her to focus on folk music. They gassed up Cass's VW bug and drove to Chicago where Tim had connections.

In Chicago they rehearsed with John Brown and sang as The Triumvirate. Making less than a hundred dollars a week and shivering through the winter months, they refined their sound and gained experience. Much later, in the early seventies while making a live recording at Mr. Kelly's, a nightclub in Chicago, Cass reminisced for the audience. She told them how glad she felt to be playing Mr. Kelly's, and how in the early 60s, her group played "basket houses," such as The Fickle Pickle, in Chicago, where the money collected in the basket that passed through the audience was shared among the singers. "…if you made six bucks, it was a good night," [4] she said.

A gig in Omaha had them following Jim Hendricks (not Hendrix.) Cass admired Jim's good looks and divine voice. Soon, he replaced Brown in the group, though she always remained friends with John Brown.

Tim Rose arranged an audition with Bob Cavallo at "The Shadows," a nightclub in Washington D.C. Broke and desperate for work, they sang poorly. Even so, Bill Cosby's manager, Roy Silver, happened to be in the club that day and saw sparks of talent. Under his management, the Triumvirate became the Big 3, destined for The Bitter End in New York City.

The Bitter End, the club that had brought recent fame to Peter, Paul and Mary, stood at the heart of Greenwich Village, the center of the folk movement. Greenwich Village harbored the clubs and coffee houses that appealed to the adventurous youth. The Big 3 lived on Bleecker Street, above The Bitter End. Wearing tailor-made outfits, they opened two or three sets each evening for other artists and comedy acts, and thrilled audiences with their harmonic folk singing,

After a few months of a successful run, Cass suffered a nervous laryngitis that interfered with her work time after time. Usually she did go on stage but Rose and Hendricks felt that she manipulated them with her complaints. Sometimes she arrived late for rehearsals not having eaten. She would say, "I can't sing if I'm hungry." Cass was the star, charismatic and charming on stage with a powerful, mellifluous voice. So they waited for her.

To keep the group together and Hendricks out of the draft, Cass and Jim Hendricks married in 1963. The marriage wasn't a true one, but the contract increased their bond of friendship. Meanwhile, Tim Rose didn't know about the wedding. He'd grown aloof from them. Feeling deprived of the recognition

Cass got from fans and feuding with her over style, Tim wanted to experiment with the blues. Cass liked the Beatles.

The recording of their songs, *The Big 3 – Live at the Recording Studio* wasn't well distributed but it was testimony to their perfect sound. They sang folk songs in one voice, pronouncing words identically in jaw–dropping harmony. Rose later quipped that they were the only folk group that sang in tune. They had worked many months together and were invited to *The Tonight Show*. Cass's career was in forward motion before the group dissolved. She was a pro with a golden voice and a few solid connections.

Cass met Dennis (Denny) Doherty at The Dugout, a bar next to The Bitter End, where performers socialized between gigs. Denny had seen Cass on stage, and was captivated by her. Instantly attracted to each other, they shared a few drinks and Cass challenged Denny,

"We're going to try and drink each other under the table, aren't we? So, let's get under the table and drink." [5]

"And that's what we did," said Denny, "under the red checkered table cloth, in the sawdust, with a bottle of Jack Daniels Green Label." [6] Denny became the most important man in Cass's life, both musically and emotionally.

Denny Doherty, from Nova Scotia, had been singing with The Halifax Three. Soon, Cass and Jim Hendricks began rehearsing with Denny, together with Zal Yanovsky on guitar, and John Sebastian on harmonica. Denny's mellow tenor voice and Cass's contralto were a perfect combination.

In the summer of 1964, the group played together as The Mugwumps at The Shadows, in Georgetown, D.C. On their record, *The Mugwumps, an Historic Recording*, Cass and Jim Hendricks had written two of the songs, "Here it is Another Day," and "Everybody's been talking."

Record companies expected artists, as the Beatles did, to compose their own songs. The Beatles loomed large over the international landscape and their appearance and melodic styles were widely admired and copied. Cass idolized John Lennon. The Mugwump men grew their hair long and so did a lot of other people. Art Stokes, an African-American drummer, joined the group, with a backbeat sound—a fusion of folk and rock. Zal Yanovsky's twelve-string guitar provided an electric twang.

Cass, the adventuress, experimented with LSD, the new hallucinogenic drug. She was evicted from her apartment where she finger-painted the wall in mustard-yellow designs. But Cass found a family in the Mugwumps. They loved each other. Never before had she known the kind of security she felt in that group and never would she have it again.

They sang only one time at the Peppermint Lounge in New York before it closed. When the Peppermint Lounge closed, Warner Brothers wanted to make a record with the Mugwumps, but they thought the female vocalist looked too stout next to the skinny guys in the group. Her manager offered to send Cass to a weight loss clinic but she declined, though she worried that her excessive poundage had interfered with their success.

The group lived in poverty at the Albert Hotel off of Washington Square. Soon, Denny had a chance to work with John and Michelle Phillips. Then John Sebastian and Zal Yanovsky formed the core of The Lovin' Spoonfuls.

During the summer of 1965, Cass went solo for a time, singing Cole Porter songs and other standards at The Shadows in D.C. Later her manager arranged a booking at a club in New York, but it didn't go well. Discouraged and longing for Denny, she took off for St. Thomas. There she found Denny vacationing and rehearsing with his new partners, John and Michelle Phillips.

John wrote and arranged their songs with occasional help from Michelle. Cass learned all the lyrics and sang along at their practices but she wasn't officially invited to join them. In spite of her melodic addition to their harmony—neither John

77

nor Michelle had strong voices–John was concerned about Cass's size and didn't see her as a suitable candidate for his group, The New Journeymen.

Denny later recalled their island adventures: singing, playing like children at the beach, floating in the cerulean sea, and tripping out on LSD. Though Cass and John irritated one another at times, Cass and Michelle hit it off from the first. Cass, hopelessly in love, waited for the day when Denny would see her as more than a friend.

When money ran out and debts to some island folk became conspicuous, they had to leave their tropical paradise for New York, only to learn that the music scene had skipped westward. Hollywood and the surfing craze had shifted the center of the popular music world to California. Cass found her friends, Jim Hendricks (to whom she was still legally married) and Vanessa, in Los Angeles and was able to stay with them. Soon Denny, John, and Michelle joined them in Hendricks' apartment, everyone poor, sleeping on mattresses on the floor. Electricity and gas had been turned off, and they had to cook on a makeshift stove, beans and franks from cans.

Into this pauperdom, Cass invited her old friend Barry McGuire to visit. He and Cass had met when he was with The New Christy Minstrels and she, with the Big 3. McGuire's "Eve of Destruction," was a current hit. He listened to their songs. Denny said that when the four of them sang together an overtone came through–"Harvey," Denny called it–a fifth voice. Barry must have heard it, because he offered to take them to his recording studio and introduce them to his producer, Lou Adler.

The singers arrived at the studio with a repertoire of music they'd rehearsed to perfection in the Caribbean. With Cass and Denny leading, the blast of harmony almost knocked Lou off his chair. He listened with his eyes closed, and when he opened them to see the mix of body types and crazy dress on top of all that resonance, he hired them on the spot to make a record. There was no more talk over whether Cass belonged with the group. Her voice had become integral to their sound, and through her connections they had gotten the audition.

Lou gave them $5,000 each and a blue Buick convertible to share. They named the car "Howard, the Bleak," and after a short stay at the Landmark Hotel, they rented a three-bedroom bungalow on Flores Street.

Riding along in Howard the Bleak, they heard a radio interview with a member of Hell's Angels during which the host inferred that the women who accompanied the Angels were less than respectable. The biker replied,

"Now hold on there, Hoss. Some people call our women cheap, but we just call them 'our Mamas'."[7] Cass jumped on that.

"Yeah, I want to be a Mama." [8]

"We're the Mamas," Michelle chimed in. The men became "the Papas." The Mamas and The Papas signed with Dunhill Records to make two albums each year for five years, not anticipating the trouble they would have fulfilling the long commitment. The first album's title, *If You Can Believe Your Eyes and Your Ears*, represented Lou's initial impression of the group when they sang for him in his studio.

Cass's parents had given her five years to succeed in show business. That deadline had not quite arrived when "California Dreamin'" climbed to the top of the charts. On March 12, 1966, while nestled in Howard the Bleak, the group heard the first few lines of their song coming over the radio and cheered jubilantly. In Boston, it became the biggest hit since "White Christmas."*

---

* In an odd juxtaposition of composers and locations, Irving Berlin had written "White Christmas" in 1938, while stuck in Los Angeles over the holidays, dreaming of a New York winter. John and Michelle Phillips composed "California Dreamin'," in 1963, during the New York Winter while longing for sunny California.

The music of The Mamas and the Papas spoke directly to hippies, rocked and jolted them and soothed them at the same time. Petite, barefooted Michelle standing next to big Cass in velvet and boots, John with a Zhivago hat, and Denny—tall, lean, and long of hair: they belted out their songs and celebrated non-conformity at a time when the youth culture called for freedom and recreation. On stage, while the others tuned instruments, Cass and Denny joked and teased one another and engaged the audience with friendly chat. When someone from the audience yelled out, "I love ya, Cass," she came right back, "Dynamite, where you stayin'?" [7]

Unbeknownst to John and Cass, Michelle and Denny had developed a flirtatious relationship during their Caribbean island indolence. When Denny told her about the affair Cass wept in misery. Both John and Cass felt betrayed and The Mamas and the Papas became entangled in emotional chaos just as success became their partner.

In spite of tensions the good songs kept coming and the money stacked up in their bank accounts almost faster than they could spend it. John's inspiration grew mainly out of the emotional dramas within the group. The feud with Michelle fueled his muse.

Cass became a bit extravagant and bought an Aston Martin sports car—she paid in cash, shocking the salesman. She loved jewelry and shopped at Tiffany's, bought herself a new wardrobe and took her sister Leah on shopping excursions for designer clothes.

The group made TV appearances and opened for Sonny and Cher at the Hollywood Bowl to great acclaim.

But the friendships among The Mamas and The Papas had vanished. For a time, John fired Michelle. Jill Gibson, Lou Adler's girlfriend, replaced her. Jill had a good voice but felt separate from the others, who worked easily together.

"If you take one voice away, you change the sound of the group," [9] said "Bones" Howe, the recording engineer. By April of 1966, another album was due on the contract with Dunhill. There wasn't much cooperation. They learned the songs the same day they recorded them, indulging in drugs and whiskey in the process.

John and Cass admired one another's talents but they were locked in a power struggle. Cass achieved the most fame among their fans but as the composer, John's pay was higher and he insisted on artistic control. John told everyone which part to sing, how loud, and which note to come in on. Cass resented his demands.

"Ah, she who makes the earth move when she walks," [10] he once said when she arrived for rehearsal. He sent her caviar, knowing she was deathly allergic to it. Such were the insults Cass took from Phillips. She ignored the stings just as she'd ignored those from classmates.

By the summer of 1966 The Mamas and the Papas had three top ten singles, including "Monday, Monday," and "I Saw Her Again." They traveled to England to perform. Cass loved "high tea," the accent–everything British. They stayed in a ritzy apartment on Berkeley Square with a view over London. Indulging her love of shopping, Cass talked Denny into buying a wolverine coat for a thousand dollars. "It'll look lovely," Cass said. "Try it on." Denny told Eddi Fiegel, the biographer of Cass Elliot, that they bought bags and bags of clothes in London. Cass scheduled an appointment for herself at the boot maker who made shoes for the Beatles.

Unfortunately, Cass caught a bad cold in London and went to bed for a day, sad that she couldn't go out on the town with the others. While at a trendy bar called Dolly's, Denny met John Lennon and invited John and Paul McCartney back to the flat to "smoke some weed." When he went to Cass's bedroom to tell her he'd brought John Lennon home for her, she thought he was teasing: "I don't feel good...Don't do that."

Denny finally convinced her of the truth and she came downstairs to meet Lennon. They hit it off, talked till dawn, and remained friends all of Cass's life.

Michelle, meanwhile, begged to be reinstated in the group. She and Phillips made up, although she'd missed the trip to England.

Sometimes, John wanted Cass to sing out with volume and force, though she tended to have a torch-song style, good for ballads and Broadway. Cass didn't want to sing "Words of Love," which John had written with Michelle in mind. Cass thought Michelle should sing it. Or Denny. Michelle and Denny both declined to sing lead so Cass relented.

"What's wrong with that take?" [11] asked Cass.

"Just do it again," [12] John said. John had Cass stand atop a grand piano to belt out the lyrics for "Words of Love." An arduous song to sing, it required a big voice and lots of breath. Cass rehearsed it repeatedly until John finally approved and until she passed out from exertion.

In November of 1966, "Words of Love" and "Dancing in the Street," were released as a single with Cass singing lead on both songs, and within a month, the record made number 5 on the Billboard Charts.

The following spring, Cass expected a baby. She feared this might be her only opportunity for motherhood and she wanted to have the baby. Cass decided to raise the child herself and to keep the identity of the father secret, a bold plan for that era. Legally, she remained married to Jim Hendricks though she lived as a single woman.

The Mamas and the Papa's called their new album, *Deliver*. "Creeque Alley," from the new album became one of their biggest hits. Named for their old street in the Virgin Islands, it's a catchy musical story of the Mamas and Papas rise to stardom.

Cass bought a house on Woodrow Wilson Drive off of Laurel Canyon, which would be her home for the rest of her life. Owen Vanessa, named after two close friends, came into the world by Caesarean Section on April 26, nineteen hundred and sixty-seven. Cass hired a nanny and a housekeeper and went back to work.

In England again, she entertained her Beatles friends in her Chelsea home and returned to London regularly. Success gave her the opportunity to cultivate friendships with other well-known musicians and she excelled at this with warmth and spirit. Whether at home in Los Angeles or in London, Cass often had a salon of musicians keeping company at her house.

John and Michelle Phillips helped organize the "Summer of Love" festival in Monterey in June of 1967. John wrote the anthem song, "If You're Going to San Francisco, (Be Sure to Wear Flowers in Your Hair,)" for his friend Scott McKenzie. At the event Cass wrapped herself in a caftan of velvet, and The Mamas and the Papas took center stage.

Otis Redding, The Who, Jimi Hendrix, The Jefferson Airplane, Simon and Garfunkel and Janis Joplin were among the performers. "Wow," said Cass, stunned by Janis Joplin's show. Twelve hundred journalists came to the celebration where attendees openly smoked pot and took drugs. After the Monterey festival of 1967, underground music moved into the mainstream.

A warm and gracious person, Cass made friends by the score. She loved people and wanted them to like her too. Most did, instantly. But one night after a show in New York, an acquaintance from high school, one who had snubbed her back then, came calling back stage.

"You didn't know me then," said Cass, "and I don't know you now." [13] She luxuriated in her stardom. Success was her cocoon and her revenge.

The Mamas and the Papas performed on July 14, 1967, in New York's Carnegie Hall. In her "finest moment," Cass sat on the apron of the stage to croon, "I Call Your Name," and the audience fell under her spell as if in a cloud of stardust.

When time came to make the fourth album, "Bones" Howe had left them, frayed by their impossible hours and a disorganized way of working. "Bones" had been their anchor. By now John had his own studio and they could make their own rules, which meant there weren't any. One or another of them arrived late to rehearse, or didn't come at all. Or they'd rehearse for a while until hunger nagged. Michelle would cook pasta for them and after a big meal late at night they didn't want to work. Cass needed royalties to pay her bills but the group couldn't muster enough enthusiasm to sing together. John hoped a trip abroad might rekindle the flame the Virgin Islands had once sparked.

In the fall of 1967, they sailed for England on *The France*. Shipmates clapped when "The Mamas and the Papas" entered the dining room; such was their fame. But the trip flopped.

Cass had lost seventy pounds and struggled to resist the nine-course food offerings. Rough weather developed on the Atlantic and Cass became hysterical when they had to wear life jackets. Hers didn't fit. Denny calmly linked two vests together so that she could feel safe. Fortunately, that storm blew over but in South Hampton police met the ship and arrested Cass for an unpaid bill during an earlier London hotel stay. Humiliated, she briefly went to jail. It became clear that the policemen's main interest concerned Pic Dawson, Cass's favorite boyfriend, who'd stayed with her in that hotel on a prior trip. They believed Cass might have known of Dawson's whereabouts. She didn't.

Cass had a final rift with John Phillips during the trip and announced the dissolution of the group in the British magazine, *Melody Maker*. She wanted to work solo.

Regardless, the group came together in John's Bel Air studio to finish the album for which they were under contract. Michelle wanted to include an older song that a friend of her father's–Favian André–had co-written. "Dream a Little Dream of Me" became Cass's signature song, and the one that would launch her solo career. She treated it like a ballad. She later told *Melody Maker*, "I tried to sing it like it was 1943, and somebody had just come in and said, 'Here's a new song.'" [14] Her personality shines through it. The record would be her biggest all-time smash, selling over a million singles in twelve weeks. For the cover image, she lay naked on her front-side in a bed of daisies.

Once, when Denny Doherty was drinking too much and his finances fell into shambles, she drove to his house and asked him to marry her. Denny loved Cass but only as a cherished friend. He declined her proposal and she lost forever the dream of Denny as sweetheart.

Over her lifetime Cass knew a succession of boyfriends and lovers. Her friends didn't usually approve of her romantic liaisons. Pic Dawson was a drug dealer. Totally enthralled by him, Cass dropped everything and everyone whenever he appeared at her doorstep, at times hiding out from Interpol or the FBI. Dawson brought hard drugs into Cass's household. The knocked-out, numbness of heroin's effects seduced Cass. In this state she escaped her weight issues and forgot the cruelty of schoolmates. She checked herself into Rehab clinics several times trying to quit heroin.

John Simon produced her solo album. Simon spent time at her house, planning the album with her, hanging around the pool, the two of them playing with Cass's daughter, Owen. Having recently worked with Janis Joplin, Simon found Cass easy to deal with. "Janis Joplin was like a tornado and Cass Elliot was a calm sea,"[15] said Simon, who made *Cheap Thrills*, for Big Brother and the Holding Company, as well as albums for Simon and Garfunkel. The recording came together in ten days. *Dream a Little Dream of Me* sold 150,000 copies, a mild success. In an interview with *Rolling Stone*, Cass expressed satisfaction with the songs selected and with the artistic achievement.

In the middle of her battle with drugs, an extravaganza—a one-woman show—was planned for Las Vegas. She now hated being called "Mama Cass" and wanted to prove she could succeed without any vestige of her former group. She would be billed as Cass Elliot.

She had resumed a four-day a week fasting diet with light meals on weekends, and lost a hundred pounds by the time she had to perform in Vegas. But she was used to singing with a talented, collaborative group and became nervous facing the solo appearance, missing most of the rehearsals. Cass opened the show with laryngitis and fever, sang flat, her voice, weak; she forgot her lines and made negative comments about The Mamas and the Papas. The half-hearted applause crushed her. She canceled the rest of the shows at Caesar's Palace, returned to Los Angeles and never got over the disgrace.

Depressed, she started eating again. Huge debts resulted from the Vegas fiasco, and she feared she'd have to return her beloved sable coat. But a new album included "Move in a Little Closer, Baby," and "It's Getting Better." Both were hits.

Cass hoped to have her own television show so that she could stay at home in Los Angeles with Owen. She appeared on The Andy Williams Show in April of 1968 as Cass Elliot. She and Andy performed a complicated duet perfectly—two consummate pros getting on the inside of their songs, making great sound with good humor. In the 70s she appeared on *The Julie Andrews Hour, The Mike Douglas Show, The Andy Williams Show, Hollywood Squares*, and *The Carol Burnett Show*. Spontaneous and warm, Cass was a popular guest. Occasionally though, she appeared in skits containing "fat lady" jokes, which mortified her. During one such sketch Carol Burnett asked,

"What are you gonna have for dinner tonight, chicken, roast or ham?" [16]

"Yeah," she replied, to thunderous laughter. She knew that size was part of her image and that she had altered forever the perception of what a "star" must look like. She had hit the top not in spite of her girth or because of it, but on the merits of her personality, talent and hard work. Cass needed TV gigs to pay her bills but the jokes about her size haunted and agonized her.

She guest hosted for Johnny Carson on The Tonight Show and appeared on his program many times. She did some acting in *Young Dr. Kildare* and *Love, American Style*. But a TV special starring Cass Elliot wasn't a big hit, and her dream of having her own show hadn't yet come true.

The brutal, bloody murders of Sharon Tate and three friends occurred on August 9, 1969. These shocked and terrified Los Angeles "society," who had visited each other's houses in an open door environment, rock stars and movie stars intermixed. Cass had been chummy with Sharon, and had to testify at trial. In the wake of the murders, the atmosphere among Los Angeles celebrity party people was never again quite so casual.

On one of the trips to England, Cass met the Baron Donald von Wiedenman, an American journalist for *The Telegraph,* who came to her hotel to interview her. She invited him to escort her to a rehearsal. Cass, who saw that some fans had noticed her, strolled across the hotel lobby in movie-star dark glasses, dragging her fur coat. Von Wiedenman watched this scene with enchanted interest. During her next trip abroad, von Wiedenman invited Cass to his home on the Riviera for a holiday.

Long after her divorce from Jim Hendricks, when Cass was at home in Los Angeles, von Wiedenman proposed marriage by phone from Europe. Cass was flattered. She wanted to please her mother and Cass thought wistfully that a father would be good for Owen. After a garden wedding in 1970, Cass became a Baroness and von Wiedenman moved into her home in Los Angeles.

Cass was still using heroin; and though von Wiedenman liked recreational drugs, he stopped short of heroin. Cass's household had become a chaotic jumble of hangers-on, some genuinely interested in friendship and music and others attracted to getting high and taking advantage of Cass's generosity. The couple fought over the general household mayhem.

Cass's friends didn't approve of von Wiedenman. They found him meek, subservient to her, and peculiarly jobless. It was finally Cass who'd had enough. She sought help for her drug problem and asked the social worker to let von Wiedenman know that she didn't have enough energy to fulfill the demands of a career while being confined in a marriage. It was a time of sadness for Cass as she went through with the dissolution of her marriage to von Wiedenman. They remained life-long friends.

Early in 1970, Cass had recorded "The Good Times are Comin'," a beautiful song by John Barry and Hal David, much suited to her voice and philosophy, for the movie, *Monte Walsh.*

In the summer of 1971, The Mamas and The Papas reunited for one last album to honor the old contract, though they'd been separated for three years. Cass was in frail health. A nurse came with her to the sessions and monitored her blood pressure. *People like Us* received the same mild interest from the public that the group demonstrated in recording it.

Over one year's time between September of 1970 to July 1971, Jimi Hendrix, Janis Joplin and Jim Morrison had all died of drug overdoses, which frightened many people sober. By September of 1971 as she turned 30, Cass engaged in intensive psychotherapy, lost weight, played tennis and "got clean." She became interested in politics and making America better. As workers in Senator George McGovern's 1972 Campaign for President, she and Shirley MacLaine warmed up crowds before Mc Govern's speeches.

Denny came by Woodrow Wilson Drive one day and asked Cass if she'd like to work–that is, sing with him again and Cass declined, though she knew they would always be friends. Cass and Michelle renewed their friendship. Michelle, now divorced from John, came by often with her daughter so that Chynna and Owen could play together.

Cass revered her family. Leah Kunkel, her sister, became a singer and songwriter. Leah said Cass was her biggest fan, and when Leah composed a new song Cass wanted to hear it, "immediately." Cass recorded two of her sister's songs beautifully in 1972, on *The Road is No Place for a Lady.* Leah wrote the title song for the album. In 2009, the recording was re–mastered by the original producer, Lewis Merenstein, in collaboration with Leah and Cass's daughter, Owen. Cass sings, "Baby I'm Yours," and "Say Hello," on the album, in addition to "It's All in the Game," among others, and on a bonus track, "East of the Sun (and West of the Moon.)" The re-mastered CD is a tribute to Cass Elliot's astonishing talent and versatility.

In June of 1972, a new road show, *Don't Call Me Mama Anymore* became a sell-out sensation. She was proud of her smash hit at The Flamingo, a solid vindication for her previous Las Vegas flop. Some of the best songs from the show were recorded live during her two-week run at Mr. Kelly's in Chicago. On the album *Don't Call Me Mama Anymore*, Cass belted out the title song, a great tune with clever lyrics, and sang "The Torch Song Medley," a sensational jazz trio, demonstrating her ability to croon the blues with vitality and glamour. She also rendered a memorable "I'll Be Seeing You." Cass could sing. She could act. She could dazzle an audience.

For the album, and the show, Roger Nichols and John Bettis wrote a song just for Cass: "I'm Coming to the Best Part of My Life." Cass met the Carpenters through John Bettis. Karen, Richard, and Cass spent a long evening together singing and harmonizing. They got along well, though Karen didn't pick up on the subtle hints through which Cass offered pharmaceutical augmentation. Cass was clean from heroin but she had returned to the use of other substances.

Owen stayed with her grandmother Bess while Cass traveled to London with *Don't Call Me Mama Anymore*. Music Director Marvin Laird and choreographer Walter Painter went along, and so did George Caldwell, chosen by Allen Carr to be Cass's tour manager.

Caldwell, tall, good-looking and assertive, sought fame as a scriptwriter and actor and plied his own interests on his time off. His job was to make sure Cass had everything she needed on stage and off. He'd managed her last few American engagements and though Cass had been ambivalent about him going on the tour, mostly because she would have to share her proceeds with him, George Caldwell had become her manager as well as her boyfriend. He indulged Cass's every whim. And Cass, always looking for the romantic rescue, hung on Caldwell's every word.

Cass asked her physician for some tranquilizers and sought advice from a specialist for a nervous laryngitis, common for her before a big performance. In the evenings before opening night she stayed at home in a comfortable flat loaned to her by a friend. She read, crocheted, and rested her voice.

The opening night audience in the Palladium saw her in a bejeweled denim dress with parasol to match, rising up on a platform from below stage. She sang for the crowd and talked with them as if they were in her living room. For her scratchy throat she kept a container of brandy mixed with orange juice on the stage piano to sip between numbers.

The audience stood up to offer their final, wholehearted applause.

After signing autographs near the stage door, she met her friends for dinner: Caldwell, Painter, Laird, and the dancers from the show. Later she celebrated with actors and singers: Ann-Margaret, Sammy Davis Jr., Ryan O'Neal and others.

"I'm in big time show biz," [17] Cass would say. The Palladium was the most majestic venue of her experience. For each show she danced and sang for seventy minutes.

"Excuse me while I stand here and breathe," she told the audience during a pause on stage. Cass had a pretty face, beautiful hair, long eyelashes, and a wonderful wit. She created an intimate atmosphere between herself and the audience, sharing a favorite recipe or confessing a prior faux pas.

She was featured in every tabloid, every newspaper. In the States, as the news of the hit show came in, Cass received offers through Allan Carr for film scripts and TV shows at home. She was excited by the possibilities.

She did have doubts about Caldwell's intentions toward her. She told von Wiedenman by phone on the evening before the last show that she thought her manager had told Caldwell to pretend to be in love with her in order to keep her happy. Von Wiedenman told her not to worry. "…you don't know anything for sure." He told her to "knock 'em dead," for the last performance.[18]

On July 27, the last night of the London performances, she did two shows—one at 6:15, and one at 8:45. The theater was full and the audiences cheered on and on. Debbie Reynolds followed Cass, and Cass wrote a greeting in lipstick for her on the dressing room mirror, "Dear Debbie, if they are half as nice to you as they were to me, you will have a great time. Love Cass."

After the last performance, she went to Mick Jagger's thirty-second birthday party in Chelsea, and on Sunday morning she attended a brunch given for her by singer, Georgia Brown. By this time people noticed Cass's hoarse voice, and that she coughed and seemed to feel unwell. But that evening she made a brief appearance at a cocktail party given in her honor by TV writer Jack Martin, and told him she'd never been so happy in her life. When she got to her flat and before she went to sleep, she called Michelle Phillips in the States to tell her about the standing ovations.

The next morning, on July 29, 1974, Dot McLeod, her London assistant, Caldwell, and others waited in the apartment for Cass so they could plan the schedule. When she hadn't appeared by mid-afternoon, McLeod went to see about her and found her in bed, cold. Then Caldwell checked her and reported to the others that Cass had died. In just two months Cass would have been 33 years old.

The post-mortem examination listed her death as a result of "fatty myocardial degeneration due to obesity." She may have had a disturbance in heart rhythm, causing death. (Cass had been hospitalized twice in 1974, for fainting spells.) No alcohol or drugs were detected.

Some of Cass's last thoughts were of Denny Doherty. Among items found in her room were liner notes she had written for the cover of Denny's new album, "Waiting for a Song," that she'd left for McLeod to type. Cass and Michelle had sung the background vocals for the album. In the notes she wrote of her long friendship with Denny, and then "...I've said what I wanted to except for one thing – he's made a super album – listen and hear for yourself. It was a long time coming–but tell me what things aren't worth waiting for." [19]

On August 3, 1974, Cass's remains were flown to Los Angeles for Jewish funeral services and cremation at Hollywood Memorial Cemetery. Her ashes were interred at the Baltimore Hebrew Congregation Cemetery. In 1991, Bess moved Cass's ashes to Mount Sinai Memorial Park in Los Angeles.

Cass's sister and brother-in-law, Leah and Russ Kunkle, took custody of seven-year old Owen Elliot and raised her along with their son Nathaniel.

Cass Elliot's life is remarkable and unforgettable, rich in beauty and song. Michelle Phillips believes that Cass's most fervent dream had come true when she won success as a solo performer.

Cass was inducted, posthumously, into the Rock and Roll Hall of Fame for her association with The Mamas and The Papas. Owen accepted the award in 1998.

Above: Mount Sinai Memorial Park in Los Angeles, California

Cass's Marker in Mount Sinai Memorial Park, Los Angeles

Cass Elliot
Bibliography:

Fiegel, Eddi. *Dream a Little Dream of Me, The Life of Cass Elliot*, Chicago Review Press, Chicago, IL: 2005

Hoskyns, Barney, *Hotel California, The True-Life Adventures of Crosby, Stills, Nash, Young, Mitchell, Taylor, Browne, Ronstadt, Geffen, the Eagles, and their many friends,*
John Wiley and Sons, Inc, Hoboken, New Jersey: 2006

Phillips, Michelle, *California Dreamin'* Warner Books, New York, NY: 1986

Unterberger, Richie. *Turn!Turn!Turn!* Backbeat Books, San Francisco: 2002

Whitburn, Joel, *Top Pop Singles 1955 – 1993* Menomonee Falls, Wisconsin: 1994

www.dennydoherty.com

www.casselliot.com

Quotes:

1 "Won't somebody please…" Page 10 – Fiegel, *Dream a Little Dream of Me*

2 "I've been fat…" Page 1 – Fiegel, *Dream a Little Dream of Me*

3 "Well, at least…" Page 42 – Fiegel, *Dream a Little Dream of Me*

4 "…if you made six…" "Cass Elliot," the CD, audience rap.

5 & 6 "We're going to…" www.dennydoherty.com

7 "Cass, I love you," Page 179 – Fiegel, *Dream a Little Dream of Me*

8 "Now hold on…" www.dennydoherty.com

9 "If you take…" Page 192 – Fiegel, *Dream a Little Dream of Me*

10 "Ah, she who…" Page 185 – Fiegel, *Dream a Little Dream of Me*

11 & 12 "What's wrong with…" Page 185 – Fiegel, *Dream a Little Dream of Me*

13 "You didn't know…" Page 219 – Fiegel, *Dream a Little Dream of Me*

14 "I tried to..." Page 243 – Fiegel, *Dream a Little Dream of Me*
15 "Janis Joplin was..." Page 252 – Fiegel, *Dream a Little Dream of Me*
16 "What are you ..." Page 307 – Fiegel, *Dream a Little Dream of Me*
17 "I'm in big..." Page 350 – Fiegel, *Dream a Little Dream of Me*
18 "you don't know..." Page 358 – Fiegel, *Dream a Little Dream of Me*
19 "I've said what..." Liner Notes "Waiting for a Song" Denny Doherty's album

More Notes – Cass Elliot

Page 71 - Bess and Philip – Page 3 – *Dream a Little Dream of Me The Life of Cass Elliot*, Eddi Fiegel, hereafter referred to as Fiegel
       Harmony singing – Page 10 and 11 – Fiegel
       The *La Boheme* performance – Page 10 – Fiegel
Page 72 - Ellen and the psychologist – Page 26 - Fiegel
       Ellen and amphetamines – Page 25 – ibid
       Bizarre clothing – Page 17 – ibid
       Working for her father – Page 22 – ibid
       Her personality and wit – Page 13 – ibid
       Outer bravado and inner sadness – Prologue xiii – ibid
       Hilltop Theatre and Ellen's participation – Page 30 and 31 – Fiegel
Page 73 - She dropped out a few months before graduation – Page 32 – ibid
       Continue at night school – Page 33 – ibid
       You let me have five – Page 35 – ibid
       Fascination with backward spelling – Page 37 – ibid
       She would need a new name – Page 36 – ibid
       Aunt Lil lived in New York – Page 37 – ibid
       Footnote – "Cass hated working for" Leah's quote - Pages 35 and 36 – ibid
       losing the part of the secretary – Page 40 – Fiegel
       Cass got a small part – Page 41 – ibid
       Philip Cohen died – Page 41 – ibi
Page 74 - Cass moved into the basement – Page 43 – ibid
       Cass would introduce the show – Page 45 – ibid
       They were both Jewish – Page 45 – Fiegel
Page 74 - Perfect pitch – Page 51 – ibid
       We packed her old VW – Page 52 – ibid

The Triumvirate it was – Page 58 – ibid

Page 75 - They kept in touch – page 66 – ibid
   Silver didn't like the name – Page 73 – Fiegel
   Cass would show up late – Page 103 – ibid
   "Let's go get married." – Page 92 – ibid
Page 76 - Hendricks music and Cass's words – Page 110 – Fiegel
Page 77 - Yanovsky's new twelve-string guitar – Page 111 – Fiegel
   Art Stokes – Page 111 – ibid
   Mustard-yellow designs – Page 113 – ibid
   Cass declined the weight loss clinic – Page 126 – ibid
Page 77, 78 - Neither John nor Michelle had naturally – Page 155 – Fiegel
Page 78 - Denny recalled their island adventures – www.dennydoherty.com
   John's credit card – Page 149 – Fiegel
   Jim Hendricks, who was – Page 152 – ibid
   "No water no gas no lights" – Page 154 – ibid
   McGuire went to the apartment – Page 156 – ibid
   Phantom overtone voice – Page 164 – Fiegel
   Barry offered to introduce them – Page 156 – ibid
   "I opened my eyes" – Page 157 – ibid
Page 79 - the blue Buick convertible – Page 159 – ibid
   the house on Flores Street – Page 161 – ibid
   If You Can Believe Your Eyes and Your Ears – Page 157 – Fiegel
   They were all sitting in Howard the Bleak – Page 175 – ibid
   In Boston – Page 175 – ibid
Page 80 - the gleaming yellow Aston Martin – Page 178 – Fiegel
   Would often take her sister – Page178 – ibid
   Friendships between them – Page 182 – ibid
   You're fired – Page 178 – ibid
Page 81 - "It'll look lovely…" – Page 196 – Fiegel
   John Lennon and Paul McCartney – Page 197 – ibid
Page 82 - debut of "Words of Love" – Page 374 – Top Pop Singles 1955-
1993 Joel Whitburn, 1994
   She found a larger exquisite Cape Cod – Page 210 – Fiegel
Page 83 - Cass gave birth – Page 211 – ibid
   Cass would come to visit London – Page 212 – Fiegel
   Cass would take center stage – Page 213 – ibid
   Cass's finest moment – Page 223 – Fiegel
Page 84 - Bones Howe had quit them – Page 224 – ibid
   Passengers broke into applause – Page 226 – ibid
   The meals were nine course affairs – Page 226 – ibid
   Interested in the whereabouts of Pic Dawson – Page 230 – ibid
Page 85 - Cass told the Melody Maker – Page 223 – Fiegel
Page 85 - One evening she drove over to Denny's – Page 245 – ibid
   During Dawson's absences – Page 259 – ibid

Page 86 - Cass skipped the Sunday rehearsal – Page 267 – Fiegel
    By the time Cass walked – Page 267 – ibid
    The specter of her Vegas ordeal – Page 273 – ibid
    She soon plunged into depression – Page 272 – ibid
    Over the next few years (TV appearances) – Page 307 – Fiegel
Page 87 - A young American journalist – Page 294 – Fiegel
    Cass resumed use of hard drugs – Page 304 – ibid
Page 88 - "She asked me to go see her shrink." – Page 313 – ibid
    they would remain friends – Page 314 – Fiegel
    Drug related deaths – Page 315 – ibid
    "…she was clean and sober"…Leah's quote – Page 319 – ibid
    "She and Shirley MacLaine…" Mc Govern's quote – Page 322 –
ibid
Page 89 - Liner notes from the CD – *Cass Elliot:The Road is No Place for a Lady*, Owen Elliot-Kugell and Richard Barton Campbell and Page 330 – Fiegel
    Liner notes from the CD – *Cass Elliot "Don't Call Me Mama Anymore* – Richard Barton Campbell and Fiegel – Page 334
Page 90 - Cass's nerves began – Fiegel
    Cass rose up Phoenix like – ibid
    A standing ovation – Page 354 – ibid
Page 90 - "Excuse me while I stand here and breathe." – Page 355 – Fiegel
Page 91 - "Dear Debbie…" – Page 358 – ibid
    Cass was feted across London – Page 359
    the standing ovations – Epilogue – Page 177 – *California Dreaming*
Michelle Phillips, here after referred to as Phillips
    In the morning, as it was Monday – Page 359 – Fiegel
Page 92 - Debunking the myths – www.casselliot.com
    Liner notes from "Waiting for a Song" Denny Doherty
    I know that when she died… Page 177 – Phillips

Discography:

The Big Three Featuring Mama Cass Rhino Entertainment Company, Collectables Narberth PA 2000
Cass Elliot The Road is No Place For a Lady   Sony Collectors Choice Music, New York, New York: 2009
Cass Elliot "Don't Call Me Mama Anymore" One Way, Albany NY BMG Special Products, 2000
Denny Doherty, Waiting for a Song, Varese Sarabande 1974

Mamas Big Ones, MCA Records, Universal City, California: 1973

The Mamas and The Papas Greatest Hits, MCA Records, Los Angeles: 1998

The Mugwumps, An Historic Recording, Warner Brothers Records, Burbank, California: 2007

Videography:

The Mama Cass Television Program, The Infinity Entertainment Group: 1969

The Monterey International Pop Festival: 2007 Razor and Tie, LTD, New York, N.Y.

Ruby Elzy 1942, (John Springer Collection/Corbis Images)

Ruby Elzy   (1908 – 1943)

In the early nineteen hundreds, the town of Pontotoc remained a peaceful oasis within Mississippi, a state teeming with racial strife. Black and white children played together in this rural mill town but blacks lived out on the edges of town and worked menial jobs for whites. Emma Elzy knew that her daughter, Ruby, would never realize her dream if she stayed in Pontotoc.

Ruby Pearl Elzy was born February 20, 1908 to Emma and Charles Elzy, the first of four children. At the age of four, Ruby accompanied her mother and her Grandmother, Belle Kimp to the McDonald Methodist Church. Emma sang with the choir near the altar and Ruby sat with her grandmother in the front pew. While standing to sing along with a spiritual, one Sunday, Ruby's sweet, powerful voice rang out above all the others in the church. The astonished congregation applauded the bright-eyed little girl. She had won over her first audience.

In 1919, eleven-year-old Ruby finished the fifth grade in the one-room schoolhouse where her mother was the only teacher. Since there was no high school for black children in Pontotoc, she puzzled over what she would do with her life.

Amanda Bell, Ruby's sister, had been born in 1909; a brother, Robert Isaac in 1911 and another sister, Beatrice Wayne (called Wayne) came along in 1912. Emma's husband, Charles Elzy, abandoned the family when Ruby was five years old.

Emma taught in the school for black children in the morning; she picked cotton in the afternoons. In the evenings, with the assistance of her mother Belle and her Grandmother Fannie, she washed clothes for white families.

Ruby worked in the family garden and helped with the younger children. As she grew older, she did the laundry with Belle and Fannie. While they folded linens, Fannie, a former slave, told Ruby stories about the great Negro Spirituals. "Steal Away," was the song the slaves sang to pass the message along between workers and from one plantation to another that there would be a meeting that night. Ruby learned "Steal Away" from Fannie and sang it as a child, while delivering her bundles of laundered linens through the meadows and lanes of Pontotoc. Later and throughout her life, she would sing it for church as well as theater audiences.

One of Ruby's best friends was a white girl, Jane Lathan, whose mother gave piano lessons to privileged children in town. Jane was permitted to play a Victrola, an early phonograph machine bearing a bell-shaped horn, which stood next to the piano in their living room. To Ruby's enchantment, Jane played records of songs that Ruby wanted to hear over and over again.

During one visit with the Lathans, Ruby overheard Jane's mother describing a concert she had attended in Memphis. Mrs. Lathan told her friends about the large hall, the singer, her beautiful gown, the program of music and an enthusiastic audience that gave standing ovations. Captivated by the image, Ruby ran home to tell Emma about it. She told her mother that this was what she wanted for her own life—to stand on a stage in a pretty dress and sing for people. She lowered her head and almost in the same breath she said, "But I know that's too much for a little (colored) girl to wish for." [1]

Emma went to the porch to compose herself and to ask God for the right words to say to her daughter. Back inside, she found Ruby weeping at the kitchen table. Emma looked in her eyes and said, "Ruby, if being a singer is what you really want, then just keep praying. And someday God will open the door for you to do it." [2]

For the Kimp/Elzy family the McDonald Methodist church was a second home, so it was natural that Emma ask her church Missionary Society to enroll Ruby in Rust College in Holly Springs, 60 miles away. Rust was one of the first colleges established for blacks in the South. It included a high school. Ruby wasn't old enough for the high school but the two head mistresses of the E.L. Rust Industrial Home for Girls agreed to admit her. Ruby could work for food and lodging, and Emma would contribute ten dollars per month for her classes. At age fifteen, Ruby would be able to enter the high school.

Alone and miles away from Emma, Belle, Fanny, and her devoted siblings, Ruby took on her new duties at the children's home at Rust. She cleaned the milk pails every morning after they had been used to milk the cows. When she entered the high school in 1923 she helped the headmistresses care for younger children at the home. In June of 1926, she graduated with honors from Rust College High School and three months later she entered the college program.

Working her way through her freshman year at Rust College, Ruby washed tablecloths for the cafeteria. (Years later, she joked on the *Fred Allen Show* she got so tired of tablecloths she never wanted to see another one. After college, a simple oilcloth covered her table at home.)

Ruby made many friends at Rust, for she was good-humored, kind, pretty and popular. Her classmates called her "Rube."

Though Rust didn't have a formal music program, a "Music-Voice" class provided an opportunity for her to sing. Dr. L.M. McCoy, President of the college, admired and supported her from their first meeting, and she performed for campus gatherings and represented the college by singing at events within Mississippi as well as in Memphis, Tennessee.

In the spring of 1927, Dr. C.C. McCracken, an educator from Ohio State University and his colleague, Dr. Walter C.

John, an administrator from the U.S. Office of Education in Washington D.C., toured southern Negro schools and colleges to evaluate them. The long series of train trips was about to come to an end, when they arrived at Rust College. While the visiting educators met in McCoy's office to complete their assessments, Ruby's clear, pure, soprano voice drifted in through the open windows with strains of "Steal Away to Jesus." The men forgot their work and asked to see the one whose voice charged the atmosphere with lyrical beauty.

Dr. McCoy walked the gentlemen to the auditorium and asked Ruby if she would mind having a small audience for her rehearsal. Standing on stage with a pianist and a violinist, Ruby greeted the strangers politely. She sang classical songs and spirituals, filling the hall with her voice. At lunch afterwards, Dr. McCoy explained to the visiting educators that Rust College couldn't properly prepare Ruby for the singing career she wanted.

Before he left the campus, McCracken told Ruby that he would arrange an audition for her at Ohio State University if she would like to try out for a program of study there.

Ruby's mother struggled with a decision to allow her daughter this trip into unknown territory for an unknown future, but Ruby wrote to her, "Mama, you said God would open a door for me. Now that he has, are you going to kick it shut or will you let me go?" [3] Emma consented and she and Ruby began a lifelong friendship with C.C. McCracken and his family.

Dr. McCoy raised funds to buy train tickets and a new outfit for Ruby's travel. She cried as she accepted the gifts, realizing how much she would miss Rust College, her second home for seven years. Ruby's teacher, Ella Becker, who had planned a vacation near Columbus, would accompany her on the train.

Late in her life, in an article for *The Etude,* a national music magazine, Ruby wrote,

"Singing was as much a part of our life as breathing. When my great-grandmother, who lived to be one hundred and six years old, got up in the morning she started to sing. She had a high, clear, soprano voice with a marvelous carrying quality, which was unforgettable. When she went to the door to greet the rising sun and thank the Lord for another day in a burst of song, the neighbors a quarter of a mile away used to say, 'All's right over at the Kimp house because Aunt Fannie's singin'. All day long as she went about her daily tasks, she would continue to sing. Thus, from my earliest hours I have been saturated with the quality and the tradition of the Negro spirituals." [A]

On the evening before the trip to Ohio, friends and neighbors filled the Kimp house. Ruby always remembered that night. "We sat on the floor, all of us. My grandmother asked me to sing 'Steal Away.' We sang our spirituals far into the night." [4]

Dr. McCracken waited at the Columbus train station, and when Ruby and Ella arrived he drove them to his house, where they met Mrs. McCracken. When Ella objected to the small attic room the family had prepared for Ruby, Dr. McCracken assured Ella that the quarters would be too warm in summer and that they were temporary. He wanted to place Ruby with a black family closer to campus. But Ruby said, "...can't I just stay here? ...I'm from Mississippi. That heat in the attic will make me feel right at home." [5] From that moment on, Ruby's joyful graciousness endeared her to the McCrackens.

Ruby first sang for Mrs. McCracken, a classically trained musician, and then for Dr. Royal Hughes, head of the music department at OSU. Both were amazed by the young woman's vocal ability and accuracy of pitch.

Subsequently, she performed at the Hughes' home for an audience of 30 accomplished musicians. One of the guests, a violinist with the Columbus Symphony Orchestra, said to Dr. McCracken, "Whatever you do, don't let that girl go back to

Mississippi. Her voice is magnificent and she has the personality to sell herself to any audience." [6]

Seeking to reassure Ruby's mother, Dr. McCracken began regular correspondence with Emma, which would continue for over 30 years.

In the first letter he *assured Ruby's mother, that her room on the second floor of their house was pleasant, that she passed the physical exam, and the IQ test, and that her voice proved to be of exceptional range and quality. He explained that some funds had been raised on her behalf when she sang privately for selected friends and musician—$35 had already been raised toward the required $100, which would cover her books and tuition for the first quarter of the college year.*

Emma wrote back saying she *appreciated all that was being done for her child, that she missed her terribly at times, but she knew that this opportunity was the answer to her prayers.*

Ruby entered Ohio State University as a sophomore. The Presser Foundation* issued one $250 scholarship to an Ohio student each year. It went to Ruby for the 1928-1929 school year, and again for 1929–1930. Julius F. Stone, one of the wealthiest men in Columbus who chaired the OSU Board of Trustees, contacted McCracken to offer any additional funds Ruby might need with the condition that his identity be withheld. She no longer had to worry about finances during her college years, and she never knew the name of her generous sponsor.

In February 1929, Ruby and sixteen other sopranos sang with the Cleveland Orchestra in the Columbus performance of Ernest Bloch's tone poem, *America.* Three days later she sang for Roland Hayes, the renowned black tenor of the day. Just a few hours after her audition with Hayes, she performed on

---

* Theodore Presser was the founder of *The Etude*, a magazine dedicated to music, which was first published in 1883 and continued until 1957.

106

radio for the first time, singing three solos with the university chorus.

Dr. McCracken oversaw her finances while Ruby learned to balance her bank account. Mrs. McCracken offered fashion tips and often sewed her concert gowns.

Dr. Hughes tutored her in voice and helped her to develop a wide range. Ruby's voice ranged from a low B to a D above high C. She became skilled in singing operatic lyric soprano, called Coloratura, and learned to read music and to sing in several languages.

Ruby helped in the household of the McCrackens, and when Mrs. McCracken's sudden illness required emergency surgery and several weeks of hospitalization and convalescence back at home, Ruby, with the help of Mrs. McCracken's parents, took care of the children and the household. Ruby felt devoted to all of the children her whole life, and they returned the affection.

In May 1930, Ruby graduated first in her class from the Department of Music at Ohio State University and gave a recital to a packed auditorium. Emma traveled by train to Columbus for the graduation and the recital. Ruby had saved the money for Emma's fare.

Ruby noticed that Emma's head was lowered during one of her songs, and after the reception at the McCracken's house following the program she asked her mother why she bowed her head during her French aria.

"Honey," said Emma, "I didn't know you could even sing in French! Mama thought you'd forgotten your words and was praying to God to help her baby to remember!" [7] They laughed all the way home.

Ruby spent that summer performing at Methodist music camps and giving concerts in Mississippi before returning to Rust College to begin teaching music. When, at the last minute, Dr.

McCracken secured for Ruby a $1200 Rosenwald Scholarship* to the Julliard School, (then The Institute of Musical Art,) Dr. McCoy canceled her teaching contract. He gave her a month's salary for travel expenses, and Ruby struck out for New York, where she moved into the Harlem YWCA on West 137th Street.

Her hopes for a classical singing career hinged on an outstanding performance at the Juilliard audition. Heading the audition panel was the dean of the school, Dr. Frank Damrosch, a superior musician, and the brother of the well-known composer and conductor, Walter Damrosch. Ruby felt nervous but she offered a short program of arias and spirituals carefully structured to her abilities and waited less than 10 minutes in an anteroom until Dr. Damrosch appeared. He said, "Miss Elzy, welcome to Juilliard." [8]

After World War I a great migration of blacks moved to the northern cities searching for jobs and for lives free from racial strife. The literary and artistic movement known as the Harlem Renaissance was flourishing when Ruby arrived in New York. Ruby entered a world rich with opportunities for talented black artists. Two brothers, James Weldon Johnson, a poet, and Rosamond Johnson, a musician, were at the core of the Harlem Renaissance. James Weldon Johnson wrote the words, and Rosamond Johnson, the music to "Lift Every Voice and Sing," which became the unofficial anthem of African-Americans. Ruby met these accomplished brothers, and Rosamond became her mentor and collaborator. In time, she would get to know many of the other singers and writers and become part of the "New Negro Movement" herself.

---

* Julius Rosenwald, a philanthropist, generously supported African-American education. Toward this effort he created The Rosenwald Fund in 1917. From the fund, fellowships were given to talented African-American writers, artists and musicians.

Ruby needed a job to cover expenses that her scholarship wouldn't pay for. She auditioned for Rosamond Johnson who hired her, after one song, to join his chorus at $25 a week. Within a week of her New York arrival, Ruby made her debut on Broadway in *Brown Buddies*, starring Bill "Bojangles" Robinson, the most famous black song and dance man in the country.

Eight times a week, she appeared at the Liberty Theater to sing spirituals in this musical review. She was the only soprano in the choir who could hit the three high Cs in the score. Her earnings paid the rent on a small apartment.

Ruby had been so eager to take advantage of performance opportunities that she took on too much. She juggled her Juilliard assignments with the Broadway gig but there was not enough time for piano practice and voice training. When *Brown Buddies* closed in January 1931, Ruby felt relief. She immersed herself completely in the musical world of the Juilliard School and loved it.

At Juilliard, her teacher Lucia Dunham stressed acting as well as singing, encouraging her students to develop a full range of stage abilities. Anne Brown, the daughter of a prominent Baltimore physician, also studied voice at Juilliard and became Ruby's friend. Both young women were African-American. Anne and Ruby became Dunham's stars. Anne spoke out against racial injustice while Ruby forgave it and prayed for those who fostered it. The two young women admired one another but sometimes competed for scholarships and jobs.

Ruby performed regularly with the Rosamond Johnson Choir and as guest soloist at Connecticut State Agricultural College, where Dr. McCracken was now president. She was grateful that her beloved McCrackens had moved close by.

The Rosenwald Foundation provided her with another scholarship for the 1931-1932 year at Juilliard.

During the summer between her first two years at Juilliard, Ruby met and fell in love with Gardner Jones, Jr., a college-educated journalist who worked for the Afro-American Journal, one of the leading Negro publications in America, published in Baltimore. Gardner was editor of their Brooklyn office.

Gardner came to every performance of *Fast and Furious* to hear Ruby sing her first Broadway solo, "Where's My Happy Ending?" In a few years, Ruby would ponder that question in her own life, but just then, she and Gardner were happy. *Fast and Furious* was billed as "A Colored Revue in 32 Scenes." Zora Neale Hurston, who wrote some sketches for the show, joined the cast, as did J. Rosamond Johnson, composer and arranger of its music. *Fast and Furious* closed after seven performances. Audiences had grown tired of the revue genre, now that new musicals such as "Show Boat" had plots and social themes.

In September 1931, Ruby and Gardner married and moved into a large apartment in Harlem, five blocks from Central Park. After Sunday church at Mt. Calvary Methodist Church where Ruby sang solos, she and Gardner took strolls and enjoyed picnics in the park. For a time she sought privacy and kept her marriage secret from the school, fearing that her marital status would jeopardize her career. Dr. McCracken's advised her to be honest with those who financed and mentored her. Ultimately, she informed Juilliard and Dunham of her marriage to Gardner.

Ruby received her diploma in voice from Juilliard in May of 1932, and took a summer job that year as music director at a Methodist camp in Bay Head, New Jersey. Her postgraduate year at Juilliard was unfunded when she took the summer job, but to her great relief, the Faculty Scholarship finally came through.

Gardner took leave from his work to spend the summer with Ruby. In a letter to the McCrackens on July 29, 1932, Ruby told them about the scholarship and,

110

" *We are having a fine time here. We live only 3 blocks from the Atlantic Ocean and can swim in the afternoon. I am just about 3 shades dark. You'd probably have to have a searchlight to see me in the daytime (smile).*

I went to Westport Connecticut Sunday July 24ᵗʰ to sing at the summer home of Miss Lillian D. Walk, who is at the head of the Henry Street Settlement House at New York. Mr. J. Rosamond Johnson and I gave the recital, a program of which is enclosed. There were about 300 guests present, among whom were Jane Addams of the Hull House, Mr. Nikolai Sokoloff, director of the Cleveland Symphony, Miss Hughes, the manager of the orchestra, Fannie Hurst, the writer and many others whose names you would know...

...My voice is fine this summer I am getting so much rest. And so much exercise too because my work gives me a lot of exercise, besides the dips I take in the afternoon."

In June of 1933, Rosamond Johnson signed with Paramount Pictures to provide music for a film version of "Emperor Jones,"* the successful Broadway play by Eugene O Neill. DuBose Heyward, an author and editor from South Carolina, wrote a prologue and screen play of the work. Paul Robeson,** who starred in the Broadway production, would recreate the role of Brutus Jones for the movie.

When "Emperor Jones" began shooting on Long Island, Rosamond was busy with another project and hired Ruby as his assistant. She took the choir through rehearsals with ease and expertise, showing the singers how to portray the scene of a Southern revival meeting. Ruby's quiet strength impressed

---

* Emperor Jones tells the story of a black porter who commits murder and escapes to a tropical island where he makes himself Emperor of the natives. Then he is murdered.

** Robeson had sung "Ol Man River" in *Showboat* on the London stage to great acclaim. In 1936, he would sing it again for the Hollywood film.

Dubose Heyward and Director Dudley Murphy, and she was cast in the small role of Brutus Jones girlfriend, Dolly.

Though not a box office success, "Emperor Jones" became a classic. Ruby was proud of her performance, loved working in the movie, and hoped for more film roles. She became friends with DuBose Heyward.

In April of 1934, Ruby received her Certificate of Maturity[·] after a recital at Juilliard, and in June she earned her graduate diploma in voice. Emma and Gardner were present for both the recital and the graduation. After these events Ruby traveled to Mississippi and gave concerts in Corinth, Holly Springs, and Pontotoc. The large, mixed audiences pleased Ruby who believed she was using her talent to bring black and white people together—for her, an important mission.

In November 1933, during Ruby's post-graduate year at Juilliard, the New York Times had announced that DuBose Heyward, and George and Ira Gershwin would make a musical of *Porgy*, Heyward's popular book and play.[·] Gershwin called the work a folk opera.

Heyward and Gershwin wanted to authenticate the story by casting black artists to play the roles. The Metropolitan Opera Company didn't hire black singers. So, when the Theatre Guild, which had produced the play, *Porgy*, offered to produce the opera with an all black cast, Heyward and Gershwin signed on.

Gershwin, who worked in New York writing the music, and Heyward, who wrote the lyrics in Charleston, mailed the

---

[·] The certificate of Maturity signaled a classical singer's readiness for a concert career.

[·] *Porgy* captures the plight of a disabled black man in Charleston, South Carolina, who moved through his Gullah neighborhood in a goat cart. The Gullahs were named for Angola, the African country from which their forebears hailed, and Heyward had become an expert on their history and culture.

libretto back and forth. Gershwin later took a two-month vacation to South Carolina and rented a cabin on Folly Island, near Heyward's cabin. Along with Heyward, Gershwin immersed himself in the culture of the Gullahs, attending their churches and celebrations, and infusing their sounds and spirit into his musical opus.

With the orchestrations almost done, Gershwin began to audition for the principal singers. Based on recommendations from Heyward and Rosamond, he invited Ruby to sing for him. Ruby arrived at Gershwin's luxurious New York apartment to perform a spiritual, "City Called Heaven." As Gershwin listened, he realized that Ruby fit the part of Serena, a devout woman of Catfish Row who prayed for the sick. She would have to be made up to appear older but she had the right voice for the role. So, on the very day of the audition and after only one song, Gershwin offered his hand to Ruby and said, "Miss Elzy, I would love for you to be in my opera." [9]

He put Ruby's classmate, Anne Brown, into the role of Bess. Todd Duncan, a professor of voice at Howard University was cast as Porgy. John Bubbles, a famous Vaudevillian would play "Sportin' Life." Gershwin personally chose Elzy, Brown, Duncan and Bubbles.*

To avoid confusion with *Porgy*, the book and play, the folk opera was titled *Porgy and Bess*. An exquisite concert performance of the opera, held at Carnegie Hall, would be Ruby's only appearance there.

The World Premier of the opera played on September 30, 1935, to rave reviews at The Colonial Theatre in Boston. Once scenes and songs were cut from the three-hour opera to get it ready for Broadway, Ruby's part retained two solos: "My Man's Gone Now" and "Oh, Dr. Jesus."

---

* Warren Coleman played the part of Crown and Abbie Mitchell, Clara. Edward Matthews would be Jake. Georgette Harvey took the role of Maria and became good friends with Ruby.

"When I came to the role of Serena, I was prepared for it," [10] said Ruby. For this, she credited Lucia Dunham, her teacher.

At the Broadway opening at the Alvin Theater, October 10, 1935, Edna Ferber, Fanny Hurst, Richard Rogers and Irving Berlin were in the audience, as were Kirsten Flagstad and Lily Pons. Gardner and Emma sat with the McCrackens and Lucia Dunham. The bravos were long and loud and the critics, mixed in their reactions to the opera, praised the cast. Ruby got some of the best reviews. *Stage* magazine's music critic, Marcia Davenport, wrote "…The singer has it. She distills heartbreak from this extraordinary piece of music…Miss Elzy is a notable artist." [11]

While some critics objected to stereotypical black roles, others insisted that Heyward's impressions accurately represented the culture of the Gullahs of that era. And *Porgy and Bess* became the most popular of all American operas internationally.

Porgy and Bess played eight times a week for a total of 124 performances. Such frequent performances with the intense vocal and dramatic exertion required for the Serena role, would be considered too strenuous today.

Ruby should have had Sunday off; instead she sang a dress rehearsal for a broadcast with Melody Master, a weekly musical radio show, and sang for the live performance as well. Her lovely voice delighted listeners across the country. Ruby had become a star.

She had a tight schedule during the winter of 1935/36. In addition to the stress of so much work, Ruby and Gardner had some disagreements, which caused her great sorrow. New York winters had never agreed with Ruby and she developed a high fever and bronchitis during the Broadway *Porgy and Bess* and had to miss a week of work. When the show traveled to Philadelphia in late January she was still recuperating.

The McCrackens had moved again, this time to Philadelphia, and they threw a party for the cast after the final performance there. But an exhausted Ruby went upstairs to lie down, unable to celebrate with her friends and colleagues. By the time the production arrived in Washington D.C. from Philly for the last stop of the tour, Ruby felt nearly normal again.

The National Theatre's policy of segregated seating caused aggravation for Anne Brown and Todd Duncan. They both had friends and family living in the area, and wanted them to be able to attend the show without being separated because of skin color. Ruby and other members of the opera company joined their protest by signing a petition. The cast would not perform unless all seats were open to blacks. Led by Anne and Todd, the effort succeeded in a historic precedent. African-Americans sat in all sections of the theater during that week. After *Porgy and Bess* closed, however, the National Theater returned to its regressive policy and until 1955, remained segregated.

In the spring of 1936, Ruby returned to New York where her marriage was disintegrating. She and Gardner had been arguing for months over money shortages, in spite of substantial incomes. There was suspicion that Gardner gambled away their assets. It's also possible that Gardner, once the main financial provider, felt diminished by Ruby's increased earnings. They couldn't patch up their differences and when Gardner left Ruby's heart was broken. Emma arrived as soon as she could to support her daughter through the darkest depression of her life. Later Ruby wrote to the McCrackens, *"Mother stayed here all summer with me, bless her. I should have died if she hadn't been with me."* [12]

In July 1937, while rehearsing for an Apollo Theater show, Ruby learned that George Gershwin had died from a brain tumor at the age of thirty-eight. With sadness, she attended the funeral of the brilliant man who had composed Serena's arias and made Ruby a star.

She participated in memorial concerts for Gershwin. The first was in New York at the Lewisohn Stadium where she sang "My Man's Gone Now" with renewed passion. She then traveled to Los Angeles to debut with the Los Angeles Philharmonic Orchestra at the Hollywood Bowl for another tribute to Gershwin. By the time she boarded the train to return to New York, she had fallen in love with Southern California and vowed to return.

Lang-Worth produced large disks called electrical transcriptions for network and local radio syndication. Several Lang-Worth Studio tracks, which aired over the radio featured Ruby. For one, she sang "Carry Me Back to Old Virginny" by James Bland; "Ring, Ring de Banjo" by Stephen Foster; and three spirituals, including "Nobody Knows the Trouble I've Seen." For another she performed Flotow's, "The Last Rose of Summer" from the opera, *Martha*; from Bohm's lied, "Still Wie die Nacht;" from Mozart's *Magic Flute*, "Ah! lo so;" and from Wagner's *Lohengrin*, "Elsa's Dream."

The recordings for the radio concerts provide a rare, enduring memorial to Ruby's haunting voice. She sings lieder, arias, blues and spirituals with equal aplomb and beauty, revealing her versatility and her lyricism–from plaintive to joyful.*

During an interval when Ruby was working a gig at the Kit Kat Club in New York, Eleanor Roosevelt invited her to sing at the White House. Each year, Mrs. Roosevelt gave a luncheon

---

* Thanks to Ruby's biographer, **David E. Weaver**, a CD exists, *Ruby Elzy in Song*. Her legacy lives on in this collection of all her recorded work. The listener enjoys Ruby's wonderful voice in a variety of songs and hears her rendition of "Summertime," from *Porgy and Bess* which she performed on the Fred Allen (radio) Show.

in honor of the Supreme Court Justices' wives. On this occasion, Ruby would entertain fifty prominent ladies following lunch in the East Room. She felt thrilled by this remarkable privilege.

Arthur Kaplan, a white pianist whom Ruby met at Juilliard, accompanied her for many concerts, including this one. Ruby and Arthur arrived at the White House on schedule. Ruby looked elegant in her white blouse and black dress with matching bolero top. Her only jewelry had been a gift from Lucia Dunham, a crystal "tear of Christ," worn as a broach. Simple and beautiful, "no fuss," as her mother would say.

The program for the event, embossed in gold, bore the Seal of the United States.

> Miss Ruby Elzy Soprano
> Mr. Arthur Kaplan at the piano
> Wed. Dec 15, 1937
> The White House

The small audience came under her spell and gave Ruby a rousing ovation. Mrs. Brandeis, the wife of a Jewish justice who had been shunned by some colleagues on the court, understood the racial barriers that Ruby encountered continuously. Mrs. Brandeis requested, "Ev'ry Time I Feel de Spirit," and Ruby sang the encore a cappella in her own inimitable style.

When Mrs. Roosevelt learned that Ruby was to sing again that evening in New York, she said to her assistant, "Have my car brought around for Miss Elzy." The chauffeur drove Ruby and Arthur to the train station. Ruby felt exultant. She and Arthur talked about their adventure non-stop on the train back to the city.

"Oh, Arthur, if only my friends back in Mississippi could see this little colored girl now." [13]

Back in New York, she discovered she'd lost her job at the Kit Kat Club, and laughed at the irony of singing at the White House and losing a job on the same day. She wouldn't miss the work, but she would miss the salary they paid her. After a few days, Emma arrived for Christmas and reminded her, "Now Ruby, you know the good lord didn't give you that beautiful voice just so you could ruin it singing in some smoke-filled nightclub to a bunch of drunks." [14]

Very soon her money worries were relieved by a telephone call. Merle Armitage, a concert and opera manager, wanted Ruby in Los Angeles in January to sing the role of Serena in a new production of *Porgy and Bess*.

Ruby and Emma celebrated Christmas in New York and the 1938 New Year in Pontotoc. At home, friends surrounded Ruby with exclamations of praise. How thrilling it had been to hear her singing over the radio–their own Mississippi daughter! Amanda and Wayne, who had followed Ruby to Rust College, were just beginning their teaching careers and had much to share with their sister. The trip was important for Ruby, who reaffirmed her roots. The journey home allowed her to view her achievements from a deeply personal perspective.

Armitage had planned this production of *Porgy and Bess* with George Gershwin before his death. Several members of the original cast collaborated to recreate the opera. Reuben Mamoulian served without pay as stage director. Armitage designed the sets and costumes, and Alexander Steinert, the original conductor of *Porgy and Bess,* took the baton. Ruby Elzy, Todd Duncan and Anne Brown shared star billing in the program. The cast included tall, handsome Jack Carr, a rich baritone, as Crown.

At the premier, floodlights beamed through the sky above the Philharmonic Auditorium. Limousines delivered the likes of Deana Durbin, Eddie Cantor, Marlene Dietrich, and Douglas Fairbanks, Jr., all well-known celebrities of the day. A crowd watched behind roped barricades as the dressed up and famous promenaded into the theater.

The entire cast saw this work as a tribute to George Gershwin. They poured their souls into their performances. Applause filled the hall while the singers gave bows. The critics raved and the grand reception elevated the status of the opera and its company.

The show proceeded to San Francisco, where Ruby celebrated her 30th birthday at a party given by Georgette Harvey. And Ruby felt wonderful.

During the third week at the Curran Theater, heavy rains and floods prevented a sell out house as well as a tour out of town. "Oh! Didn't it Rain?"* would have been an appropriate musical comment. The show closed early in San Francisco and while it was a critical success, receipts fell short.

Still, Ruby was happy. No longer brooding over her divorce from Gardner, she loved the weather in California, where she stayed healthy and free of bronchitis. She wanted to live in California and find work as a movie actress.

With this goal, she headed for Los Angeles, visited casting agents, and won a small part in the movie *The Toy Wife*. Clarence Muse, a member of the cast, who also composed and choreographed for the stage, had helped to write Louis Armstrong's theme song, "When its Sleepy Time Down South."

Muse selected Ruby to star in a play he would direct in Los Angeles for the Federal Theatre Project.* He gave Ruby the part of Ella Jones in *Run Little Chillun,* which opened at the

---

* "Oh! Didn't It Rain?" a spiritual about the biblical flood, is one of the selections on the CD, *Ruby Elzy in Song.*

* The Federal Theatre Project, a program of the Works Progress Administration, allowed artists of all disciplines to gain employment during the Great Depression while providing cultural experiences for large numbers of people.

Mayan Theatre in July 1938 to eager audiences and sensational reviews—a hit.

Run Little Chillun provided the perfect chance for Ruby to sing, "Nobody knows the Trouble I've Seen," and other beloved spirituals she knew from childhood. The musical ran for nearly a year and Ruby experienced the comfort of financial security.

She rented a Spanish style stucco house in south central Los Angeles in an upper-middle-class black neighborhood. The living room held a grand piano. Emma came to visit. Ruby's sister, Wayne, told Ruby's biographer, David E. Weaver, that this was a happy time for Ruby. "She loved the weather, the people, and living close enough to the ocean that she could swim almost every day." [15]

Because of her nightly theater schedule, Ruby attended any parties on Sunday afternoons. She made friends with other black actors in Hollywood, and was often invited to social events with Hattie McDaniel, Clarence Muse, and Florence Cole Talbert, an opera singer. Talbert encouraged Ruby never to let die her dream to sing on the grand opera stage.

On Easter Sunday, 1939, Marion Anderson, the world-renowned African-American singer, gave her historic open-air concert at the Lincoln Memorial.[*] Anderson's voice reverberated from the steps of the Lincoln Memorial for 75,000 people and for millions more over the radio.

[·] She did have sad times in 1938. James Weldon Johnson was killed that summer, when a car in which he traveled collided with a train. Six months later, Ruby's voice teacher at Ohio State, Royal Hughes died at the age of 54 from a massive heart attack.

[*] Anderson planned to appear at Constitution Hall but the Daughters of the American Revolution refused to give her a concert date. Eleanor Roosevelt, a champion of civil rights, resigned her membership in the DARs in protest, and helped Marion find a dignified place to sing. Sixteen years later, Anderson became the first black artist to perform on New York's Metropolitan Opera stage.

Once *Run Little Chillun* closed, Ruby traveled east again to play opposite Paul Robeson in a musical about *John Henry*, a folk hero. She had two solos in the show: "Careless Love" and "Lullaby," and she sang a duet with Robeson. Reviews praised both stars but the show closed after seven performances due to financial shortages. A disappointed Ruby considered her options. It was February 1940. She turned down opportunities in New York to return to Los Angeles and to Jack Carr.

Eight years older than Ruby, Jack hailed from North Carolina and had served in World War I. After the War, he began singing and acting. Though he played Jim for the original *Porgy and Bess*, Ruby had been married to Gardner at that time. It wasn't until the 1938 Armitage production of the opera that Ruby and Jack started dating. Soon after her return to Los Angeles, Ruby and Jack Carr married and he moved into her house on East 54th Avenue.

To Ruby's delight, her school-aged nephew moved in for a few months. Having no children of her own, Ruby adored Buster's presence in her household. Emma lived with them, too, most of the time. Buster reported that they would hear Jack Benny's sidekick, "Rochester," over the radio on the Jack Benny Show in the evening, and that Eddie Anderson ("Rochester,") a friend of Ruby's and Jack's, might well appear the next day at the Elzy/Carr house in person.

During the winter of 1940/1941, Ruby spent two months in Mississippi, and gave concerts in Corinth, at Rust College and in Pontotoc, where the new high school auditorium was filled to capacity. The town's newspaper headlined with, "Triumphant Ruby Elzy Comes Home." [16]

While in Pontotoc, Ruby ran into her childhood friend, Mildred, outside the Post Office.* They stopped to chat.

---

* The Town Square Post Office, "America's only full service museum exhibit," still exists in Pontotoc and contains The Pontotoc County Historical Society, a Pontotoc Museum, a Ruby Elzy Museum, and a gift

Mildred's 9-year-old son, Walter Bates, who stood with his mother on the Post Office steps, had never seen a fur coat on anyone. After they said goodbye and walked away, Walter asked his mother about the beautiful woman in the big coat, which he thought might have been a bearskin. Mildred told Walter that he had just met the famous soprano "from right here in Pontotoc." Walter, still living near the McDonald Methodist Church, in Pontotoc in 2009, said he never forgot his encounter with Ruby Elzy.

During Christmas of 1941 the acclaimed movie "Birth of the Blues" opened, starring Bing Crosby, Mary Martin, Ruby Elzy and Eddie Anderson. Critics lauded Ruby's performance. "In this cast is Ruby Elzy, whose rendition of "St.Louis Blues" will be remembered as long as the song will live." [17]

Turning down film opportunities, she accepted the role of Serena in Cheryl Crawford's *Porgy and Bess*. Crawford, a distinguished Broadway producer, assembled as many of the original cast as she could. Trimmed in length by 45 minutes, with an orchestra cut by half and production costs slashed, the opera was lean and affordable. Jack played Crown in this Maplewood, New Jersey offering, which drew New York audiences like a magnet for the summer season. The composer and critic, Virgil Thomson wrote, "Miss Ruby Elzy, as Serena, gives the single loveliest performance in the cast." [18]

Crawford took the opera to the Majestic Theatre in New York, where Ruby played the role of Serena at $200 a week and Jack sang the part of Jim at $50 per week. For the long run of the show they could be together, the only married couple in the cast. A three-week run in Boston prior to the Broadway opening covered the entire production costs–finally a profitable *Porgy and Bess*.

---

shop. Volunteers from the Historical Society work the decades old mail desk performing postal services for the citizens of Pontotoc.

Ruby was busy with eight performances a week. World War II was on. She gave concerts to raise money for War bonds and visited hospitals and military forts to entertain soldiers, particularly those of her own race.

When a critic commented on her weight gain, she decided to increase her strength for a demanding schedule with diet and exercise. In the summer of 1942, slim and beautiful, she wore a silver gown for a photograph by James Abresch, who shot another photo of Ruby in costume for *Aida*.

Porgy and Bess closed on September 26, 1942, after 286 shows. It had been the longest running Broadway revival that year. The National Tour opened two days later in Rochester, New York.

When the tour arrived in Chicago, it had already ripped through five cities. Etta Moten, an old friend of Ruby's, replaced Anne Brown in the cast. On New Years' Eve, 1942, Ruby, Jack, and Emma celebrated happily as guests of Etta and her husband, Claude Barnett, the founder and president of the Associated Negro Press. This would be Ruby's last New Year's Eve on earth.

After Chicago, Ruby and Jack traveled with the show to St. Louis. Ruby's father, Charles Elzy, lived in St. Louis, and so did her Aunts Ada and Amanda. Ruby sent tickets for all. Thirty years had elapsed since her father deserted the family, but she had forgiven him. The aunts brought Charles to the American Theatre for *Porgy and Bess*, and afterward, in Ruby's dressing room they talked a bit and Charles met Jack. As the family rose to leave, Ruby and her father embraced. Ruby said to her aunts,

"Thank you for coming and thank you for bringing Daddy, too." [19]

Following St. Louis, the troupe played Kansas City, Minneapolis, St. Paul, and Milwaukee. Closing night in Milwaukee fell on February 20, Ruby's 35th birthday. The following Saturday, in Detroit, she played her 700th performance as Serena but she didn't feel like celebrating. A year ago she had lost weight and felt fine; now she was tired and irritable.

Tests and x-rays by a Detroit physician revealed a benign tumor in her uterus, which caused increased menstrual flow, anemia and fatigue. She needed to have the tumor removed surgically but Dr. Owen agreed to treat her with medications and postpone the operation until her tour with *Porgy and Bess* ended, four months hence.

Ruby went on to Indianapolis, Toronto, Pittsburgh, and Philadelphia. Three weeks in Philadelphia brought Ruby together with Wayne, who lived in Trenton with her husband, Harry Reynolds, a soldier at Fort Dix. Wayne came to several performances and she and Ruby spent many days together. Ruby gave her one of the new publicity photos, signing, "To my precious baby sister, Wayne Elzy Reynolds, with loads of love and affection. Your Ruby." All her life, Wayne kept Ruby's picture on her dresser.

From Philadelphia, the show went to San Francisco and Los Angeles. Ruby sang at Wesley Methodist, her former church in Hollywood. She never refused the Methodists.

"I want to sing. It's my way of saying 'Thank You' for the chance God gave me through the church…" [20] Many of Ruby's friends came to the Los Angeles performance.

The show took Ruby and Jack from Los Angeles to Portland, to Oakland and finally to Denver from June 16 to 19. Frances Wayne's critique for the Denver Post includes,
"…Ruby Elzy as Serena lifts her voice in the spiritual 'My Man's Gone Now'…giving a stinging reality to the finality of death." [21]

The tour was over. Ruby, exhausted and still suffering the effects of the tumor actually looked forward to going to the hospital. Ruby, Jack and Emma made the train trip to Detroit and reported on June 25 to Parkside Hospital, one of two hospitals in the city serving only blacks.

Detroit race riots had recently killed almost 50 and wounded 700 others. The injured filled the hospitals and medical resources were stretched. Unbeknownst to Ruby, Parkside Hospital was known locally as "the place you go to die."

A month later, Emma wrote to Dr. McCracken that the night before her surgery Ruby talked about her love for his family. Emma shared in the letter all she could remember of Ruby's words on that evening.

Ruby praised Dr. McCracken and his family. She talked about what was important to her in life, what she would like to leave, from her personal belongings to each family member. Ruby told Emma how much money Jack would need for extra expenses. She joked and laughed with Jack. She said if anything happened, she was a pretty good Christian and that she loved the Lord and everything would be all right. Emma said she (Emma) just couldn't deal with anything suggesting that Ruby wouldn't get through the surgery.

When Ruby's stretcher was taken to the area where she awaited surgery, Jack and Emma left to have lunch. The operation was to be routine so they weren't worried. But they returned to tragic news. Emma and Jack stood outside the room where Ruby's body lay, holding each other and sobbing. Ruby had perished. In Emma's letter to the McCrackens, she wrote,

"They had finished the operation and were sewing her up and she just quit breathing. They said she asked for a glass of water and they told her she couldn't have the water and she quit breathing. They did everything in man's power but nothing helped."

Ruby Elzy died June 26, 1943 at 12:18 PM. She was 35 years old. Her husband Jack signed the death certificate. The causes of death were listed as "cardiac dilatation" and "shock following operation."

For Emma, if Ruby had passed away, God had to have had a hand in it. Now Emma wanted to get her baby home to the Mississippi hills where she belonged.

Ruby's funeral service took place at McDonald Methodist Church in Pontotoc. Emma sat with Jack and her surviving children in the front pew. Charles Elzy arrived to honor his oldest daughter. Dr. McCoy gave the eulogy and the Rust College a cappella choir led the singing. The pews were filled. Ruby would have smiled at the ethnically diverse congregation. Emma wrote the epitaph for Ruby's monument.

Ruby Elzy
February 20, 1908
June 26, 1943
"Now Singing in the Celestial Choir"

Ruby's death was reported through every major newspaper in America and condolences for the family arrived from friends and co-workers throughout the country.

Ruby Elzy had written an article for *Etude* magazine before she died, and it appeared posthumously in August 1943. In "Spirit of the Spirituals" she wrote,

"There's no color to talent. All success is a matter of hard work, talent, and persistence." [B]

She'd proven it in Mississippi, at Ohio State University and The Juilliard School, over the radio, and in theaters and concert halls throughout the land. With her enchanting voice and gentle good will she shattered walls that confined her people. She and her colleagues blazed a brighter, broader path for black artists who followed them.

In April of 2000, Ruby was inducted, posthumously, into the Classical section of the Mississippi Musician's Hall of Fame. Along with Leontyne Price and Elvis Presley, she was among the first twenty-seven inductees into the new organization.

But Ruby's story had been drifting into oblivion until *Black Diva of the Thirties, The Life of Ruby Elzy,* a complete biography of her life, was compiled and written by David E. Weaver and published in 2004, by the University Press of Mississippi.

The events of Ruby's life as recorded here, are taken from *Black Diva of the Thirties: The Life of Ruby Elzy.* The summaries and extractions from the letters, which appear in italics, are taken from the same book. See the Endnotes.

Ruby's Gravestone in the Pontotoc City Cemetery in Pontotoc, Mississippi, with an epitaph written by Emma, etched below the dates.

"NOW SINGING IN THE CELESTIAL CHOIR"

Ruby's Historical Marker in the Pontotoc City Cemetery

Ruby Elzy

Bibliography:

Durham Frank *DuBose Heyward The Man Who Wrote Porgy*, The University of South Carolina Press/Columbia: 1954

Etude Magazine August, 1943: Elzy, Ruby "The Spirit of the Spirituals: Religion   and   Music   a   Solution   of   the   Race Problem"

Ewen, David *A Journey to Greatness: The Life and Music of George Gershwin*, Henry Holt and Company/New York: 1956

Hutchisson, James M. Editor, *A DuBose Heyward Reader* The University of Georgia Press/Athens: 2003

Hutchisson, James M. *Dubose Heyward: A Charleston Gentleman and   the   World   of   Porgy   and   Bess*, University   Press   of Mississippi/Jackson: 2000

Weaver, David E., *Black Diva of the Thirties: The life of Ruby Elzy*, University Press of Mississippi/Jackson: 2004

Quotes:

The following quotations are taken from:
Weaver, David E. *Black Diva of the Thirties: The life of Ruby Elzy.*
1 "But I know…" page 2
2 "Ruby, if being…" page 2
3 "Mama, you said…" page 30
4 "We sat on…" page 32
5 "…can't I just…" page 35
6 "What ever you do…" page 37
7   " 'Honey' said Emma…" page 54
8 "Miss Elzy, welcome…" page 59
9 "Miss Elzy, I…" page 84
10 "When I came to…" page 85
11 "The singer has it." Page 91
12 "Mother stayed here…" page 104

The following quotations are taken from:
Etude, August 1943 "Spirit of the Spiritual"
A – "Singing was as much a part…"
B - "There's no color to talent."

More Notes – Ruby Elzy

Page 101 – An oasis – Page 12 – *Black Diva of the Thirties: The Life of Ruby Elzy*, David E. Weaver, 2004, hereafter referred to as Weaver
        On the outskirts – Page 9 – Weaver
        Emma Elzy realized – Page 19 – ibid
        Emma…sang in McDonald's choir – Page 9 – ibid
        It was little Ruby – Page 9 – ibid
        In 1919 Ruby finished – Page 18 – ibid
        more babies – Page 11 – ibid
        He never came back – Page 15 – ibid
Page 102 - Her mother's main helper – Page 16 – Weaver
        The great Negro spirituals – Page 17 – ibid
        Jane Lathan – Page 18 – ibid
        Same records over and over – Page 18 – ibid
        Mrs. Lathan described the beautiful – Page 19 – ibid
        Ruby breathlessly told Emma – Page 19 – ibid
        She went quickly – Page 19 – ibid
Page 103 - 60 miles northwest of Pontotoc – Page 19 – Weaver
        the two women decided – Page 20 – ibid
        cleaning the pails – Page 21 – ibid
        Ruby remained at Rust – Page 23 – ibid
        she was a young beauty – Page 23 – ibid
        "Rube" – Page 23 – ibid
        she represented the college – Page 24 – ibid

Page 104 - a commission to study – Page 26 – Weaver
a beautiful soprano voice – Page 26 – ibid
"if you don't mind…" Page 27 – ibid
We don't have – Page 27 – ibid
"Ruby, if I could arrange it…" Page 28 – ibid
Emma was upset – Page 29 – ibid
With Emma's approval – Page 30 – ibid
Faculty took up a collection – Page 30 – ibid
Ella Becker would soon – Page 30 – ibid
Page 105 - there he was at Union Station – Page 34 – Weaver
A room in the attic – Page 34 – ibid
The following night Ruby sang – Page 36 – ibid
Page 106 - McCracken began writing – Page 37 – Weaver
McCracken's letter to Emma – Pages 37 & 38 – ibid
Emma's letter to McCracken – Page 39 ibid
Ruby received the first – Page 49
Stone had anonymously – Page 49 – ibid
On Feb 4, Ruby – Page 47 – ibid
Ruby sang for Hayes – Page 47 – Weaver
Ruby sang three solos – Page 48 ibid
Page 107 - Cleo McCracken's surgery – Page 41 – Weaver
Ruby's graduating recital – Page 53 – ibid
Ruby had saved – Page 53 – ibid
Ruby's performances – Page 55 – ibid
"Mr. Embree's promise – Page 58 – ibid
Page 108 - Dr. McCoy kept his promise – Page 58 – Weaver
Frank Damrosch and Walter Damrosch – Page 58 – ibid
One song was all it took – Page 61 – ibid
Ruby Elzy stepped on stage – Page 61 – ibid
Page 109 - High notes were no problem – Page 61 – Weaver
Her own apartment – Page 61 – ibid
Ruby was relieved – Page 61 – ibid
Lucia Dunham – Page 62 – ibid
Anne Wiggins Brown – Page 62 – ibid
Ruby tried to understand – Page 62 – ibid
Ruby had fallen in love – Page 68 – ibid
Page 110 - Gardner came to every performance – Page 70 – Weaver
During the show's run – Page 70 – ibid
For Ruby to have been out of touch – 68 – ibid
It was true, Ruby had not told… – Ruby – Page 72 – ibid
On May 31, – Ruby graduated – Page 72 – ibid
While they were in Bay Head – Page 73 – ibid
Pages 110 & 111- Ruby's letter – Pages 73&74 – ibid

Page 117 - It was Arthur Kaplan – Page 5 – Weaver
"That won't be necessary…" - Mrs. Roosevelt's response – Page 8
– ibid
Ruby laughed – Page 123 – ibid
Finding another singing job – Page 124 – ibid
Page 118 - Could she be out in Los Angeles – Page 125 – Weaver
It had been three years – Page 126 – ibid
…great cast, Armitage also – Page 127 – ibid
When Armitage offered Carr the role – Page 127 – ibid
The scene outside the Philharmonic – Pages 129&1130 – ibid
That feeling was shared – Page 129 – ibid
Page 119 - Georgette Harvey threw a surprise – Page 132 – Weaver
"The worst flood in years" – Page 132 – ibid
She had grown as a singer – Page 131 – ibid
A small role – Page 134 – ibid
One of his tunes – Page 135 – ibid
He had found the perfect – Page 136 – ibid
Show how the Negro spiritual – Page 136 – ibid
Footnote – The Federal Theatre Project – Wikipedia
Page 120 - After nearly a year – Page 138 – Weaver
The residence at 898 – Page 138 – ibid
leading black film and radio – Page 140 – ibid
Ruby's long held dream – Page 140 – ibid
Contralto Marion Anderson – Page 143 – ibid
When the opportunity came – Page 147 – ibid
Ruby decided against – Page 152 – ibid
Footnote - The news broke that James – Page 139 – ibid
Footnote - Her beloved teacher (Dr. Hughes' death) – Page 139
– ibid
Second Footnote – It was Eleanor Roosevelt – Page 144 – ibid
Page 121 - Eight years her senior – Page 152 – Weaver
It was during that 1938 – Page 153 – ibid
Ruby returned to Los Angeles Page 153 – ibid
the little boy – Page 154 – ibid
"I'd be listening…" – Page 154 – ibid
Walter Bates Interview with the author 2009
2009 author visit to the Town Square Post Office in Pontotoc
Page 122 - Soon after returning to Hollywood (Birth of the Blues) Page 158
– Weaver
Crawford had fallen in love – Page 164 – ibid
Crawford reduced the number – Page 164 – ibid
Crawford agreed to – Page 166 – ibid
Entire cost was covered – Page 167 – ibid
The U.S. Treasury Department – Page 168 – ibid

Discography:

Gershwin Performs Gershwin Rare Recordings 1931-1935 Amerco, Inc., MusicMasters, Ocean, New Jersey 1991 BMG Music
Ruby Elzy in Song, Weaver, David E., Producer, Rare Recordings (1935-1942) Cambria Master Recordings, Lomita, CA: 2006
Decca presents selections from George Gershwin's Folk Opera, Porgy and Bess Broadway Gold MCA Classics, Universal City, CA 1992,1992,1959,1940,1942
(Ruby Elzy doesn't sing on this CD, but Todd Duncan, Anne Brown and others from the original cast do.)

Videography:

Birth of the Blues
The Emperor Jones
Tell No Tales
The Toy Wife
Way Down South

Janis Joplin in performance 1969, (Bettmann/Corbis Images)

Janis Joplin   (1943 – 1970)

"…I'd rather have ten years of super-hyper-most than live to be 70 sitting in some goddamn chair watching TV." [1] Janis Joplin enjoyed such daring proclamations. With this one, she charted her course.

Weighing five and one half pounds, Janis Lyn Joplin was born in Port Arthur, Texas on January 19, 1943, the first child of Dorothy and Seth Joplin.   A sister Laura, and a brother Michael, came later. Janis accepted them eagerly and for the most part her early years went by peacefully, but Dorothy Joplin said Janis always needed more attention than the others.

Janis grew up painting, drawing, and singing in church and with the school glee club. She won a journalism award and illustrated her school's literary journal.   In her teens she listened to folk music and blues, especially that of Lead Belly, Bessie Smith and Odetta. She mimicked their singing voices.

The   Joplins   encouraged   their   children   to   think independently and to pursue and improve their natural talents. Lively discussions took place in the home, where the entire family debated the issues of the day around the dinner table.

Janis described her early childhood as idyllic. "Then the whole world turned on me," [2] she said.   By tenth grade she hung out with the intellectual rebels, the fringe element. They copied the beatniks*and defied the conventional mores of Port Arthur social life. While she wanted to be liked, she lacked the

---

* The writings of some post World War II authors inspired the culture of the beatniks, who embraced alternative sex practices, experimentation with drugs, and spontaneous creative activity. They rejected materialism. Janis especially admired author, Jack Kerouac. His book, *On the Road*, influenced her considerably.

charm expected of young ladies in East Texas in the late 1950s and early 60s. She thought integration of the races was okay and said so publicly, not a popular stance. When classmates rebuked her for it she took to dressing in mostly black clothing, spitting cuss words and longing for "the Beat life." Add to her rebelliousness her teenage awkwardness, pudginess and severe acne, and you have Janis, who cursed and stomped and suffered insults from her schoolmates.

Though she had girlfriends Janis preferred the company of boys. Her best friend Jim Langdon, a trombone player, admired her brazen language and enjoyed her company. Janis was accepted into his group of guys. They hung out together, climbed the neighborhood bridges and towers, and listened to jazz, blues and folk music.

Janis once swiped a family car to travel to New Orleans with her buddies to bar hop and hear jazz. A wreck on the way home resulted in the ruination of the old car, a Willys. Its occupants were hauled in to the Kenner police station. Janis was not yet 18, so the police contacted the Joplins, who wired money for her bus-ride home. The boys hitchhiked.

As her sister grew older it became obvious that Laura would fall into the "normal" category. Janis saw Laura gaining respect from their mother and father even as the gulf widened between her parents and herself.

Port Arthur is an oil-refining town. Seth Joplin worked for Texaco. In the evenings, Janis often met and chatted with her father on the front porch until Dorothy overheard a conversation. Seth was telling Janis about making bathtub gin during his college days. Dorothy scolded her husband, who was crushed. The meetings stopped. Janis was puzzled and upset about losing this connection with her dad.

There had been a piano in the house. But Dorothy, who once had a fine singing voice and sang professionally, required surgery on her throat. The surgery destroyed her voice and Seth had the piano removed. Seth thought it would agonize his wife to hear Janis making music when his wife could no longer sing.

Though her grades were excellent, Janis sometimes skipped school her senior year to lounge around The Sage, an offbeat coffee shop. Some of her paintings sold at The Sage and she sang there for the clientele.

She graduated from Thomas Jefferson High School in May of 1960 and enrolled at Lamar State College of Technology in nearby Beaumont. About that time she was hospitalized after a drinking binge and saw a psychiatrist in Port Arthur. Later she would say, "I was treated for alcoholism when I was seventeen." [3]

In the summer of 1961, Dorothy persuaded Janis to go to Los Angeles and live with her aunts, Barbara and Mimi, Mrs. Joplin's sisters. Janis got a job as a keypunch operator with the telephone company. She loved her aunts but when she had saved enough for an apartment, she defied them and moved to the low-rent Venice suburb of Los Angeles. Venice had been the home of the Beatniks, who expressed anti-establishment individuality with art and poetry. They listened to blues and folk music, smoked marijuana, and celebrated their free spirits. But by the time Janis reached Venice it had become a slum. Many "artists" had moved out because of muggings, murders and drug deals.

And so the spring of 1962 found Janis back at Lamar College studying for classes, working in a restaurant, and singing at a local coffee shop as well as the Purple Onion, a folkie club, in Houston.

That Summer Janis entered the University of Texas at Austin as an art major. The night after she arrived in Austin she sang with Powell St. John and Lanny Wiggins–The Waller Street Boys. St. John played harmonica and Wiggins played bass. With Janis they formed a trio. On Wednesday nights the group performed at Threadgill's, a student bar. On Sunday afternoons they played at the Union Building where folk singers came together. Janis sang, "This Land is Your Land," "Careless Love," and "Out on Black Mountain." Sometimes she accompanied herself on an auto-harp, a kind of zither for playing chords. Onstage she was shy and not yet certain of her style. Offstage she was rowdy, "in a frenzy," said a friend, "about to explode."

The rebels hung out at "The Ghetto," a grimy boarding house near the U.T. campus. Janis spent her spare time there with some staff members of the campus magazine, *Texas Ranger* and various other community "beatniks." Her friends liked raw folk music while the "normal" crowd listened to the New Christy Minstrels and The Kingston Trio.

Redheaded Chet Helms, once an engineering student at U.T., wanted out of Texas during the civil rights movement and landed in San Francisco. He encountered Janis at Threadgill's during a return trip to Austin and found her wild and free, "one of the guys." He knew she would find an audience in San Francisco and encouraged her to travel west with him. Janis sang a final performance at Threadgill's early in 1963. Ken Threadgill, the owner and country-singing bar tender, loved Janis and shared a lifelong friendship with her.

While hitchhiking westward, the two stopped at Chet's parent's house in Fort Worth where they planned to spend the night. Janis swore openly. She looked grubby, the top buttons of her shirt were unbuttoned and she wore no bra. Chet's parents didn't invite them to stay.

Back on the road together, truckers picked them up. The cross-country trip gave them time to discuss their aversion to religion and its puritanical nature. Chet admired Janis' intelligence. Janis confided that she'd never before hitchhiked more than twenty miles from home and Chet realized that his bold and outrageous traveling companion felt terror at the prospect of leaving Texas in the distant dust.

On her first night in San Francisco Janis crooned at Coffee and Confusion on Upper Grant Avenue, where she earned a stack of coins, collected in a hat passed through the audience. Flat broke after the trip, she and Chet welcomed the little fortune. Janis settled in North Beach where many poets and artists hung out and she made money singing at the Coffee Gallery, a popular bar for the counter culture folkies. She was actually too young to work there but the owner hired her because the customers loved her. Other performers included Bobby Neuwirth, David Crosby and James Gurley. Janis wore thrift store clothes and beads and celebrated each day as though it was New Year's Eve. North Beach was a free wheeling community where she could drink, take amphetamines and explore her sexuality with girls as well as guys. She had found her place.

No one knows which drugs Janis started using or when. In Texas, she'd combined Seconal with alcohol and had taken wild walks down the middle of the streets trying to get run over. It's believed that she began using speed (amphetamines) during her first sojourn in San Francisco and that her heroin problem developed during her 1966 trip west. Between 1963 and 1965, she bounced back and forth between New York and San Francisco, drinking, shooting speed, living off of public handouts and singing gigs and having sexual adventures at will. Her favorite song was "Searchin'," by Leiber and Stoller. One night, walking out of the closing Anxious Asp barroom in San Francisco, a gang of bikers assaulted her verbally and when she sassed them they beat her up badly.

Chet Helms later said that Janis was more focused, at that time, on her drug habits than any career. RCA Records executives heard her sing and wanted to record her, but she was recovering from the bruises the bikers left her with and lost the opportunity.

Some of her acquaintances had overdosed on amphetamines and died. Feeling frightened and out of control, Janis tried to commit herself to San Francisco General

Hospital. "I'm crazy," she told them, but they thought she was a freeloader and turned her away. Indeed, she was living in Washington Square Park or in cheap Broadway boarding houses. Her weight dropped to 88 pounds and according to Chet, she had lost all ability to function rationally. Friends threw a "bus fare party" to buy her a ticket home.

When Janis returned to Port Arthur that summer, she lived at home and enrolled at Lamar College. Planning to enter "a helping profession," she majored in Sociology. For Janis it seemed that only the extremes were possible. She could take herself way beyond the edge of the mainstream or exist rigidly within it. Determined to steer clear of drugs and alcohol, she avoided anyone who looked to be a part of that scene. Staying close to home during most of 1965 and having therapeutic sessions with a social worker, she felt safe. She dressed conservatively. She arranged her hair in a bun and covered the track marks on her arms with long-sleeved dresses. She didn't sing.

Perennially empty and lonely, she saw marriage as a part of the life style she needed to stay sober. Sweet images of life included husband, family and home—all the values her mother cherished. Unfortunately, Peter, her friend from San Francisco, already had a wife. Regardless, he appeared in Port Arthur, met her family and asked her father for Janis's hand in marriage. Though Janis stitched a quilt for her trousseau and she and Peter exchanged letters for a while, he ended the relationship. The wedding was off.

With love passing her by, Janis yearned to sing. Standing in the stage-light, wailing the blues, she connected with the world and expressed her very essence. Only an adoring audience could restore her hope for fulfillment.

When she performed at the Half Way House coffee house in Beaumont, Jim Langdon was there. In his column, " Jim Langdon's Nightbeat," a music review for *The Austin American-Statesman*, Jim described her as "the greatest white female blues singer in America." [4] Dorothy was upset by Jim's reviews, fearing they would encourage her daughter to reenter the music world with all its risks.

Janis had been drug free for a year when she moved to Austin in 1966. Jim Langdon tried to convince her to remain in Austin and arranged some bookings for her. But her friend Chet Helms lured her back to San Francisco. Chet's psychedelic band, Big Brother and the Holding Company, needed a vocalist.

Though terrified of the music world's drug culture and of temptations she'd face, her passion to perform trumped her fears. Her social worker thought her awareness of the danger of drugs would save her. He encouraged her to follow her dream and to find another therapist when she got settled. Chet promised a bus ticket home if she failed.

Janis sought her family's blessing and told her mother she wanted to sing Blues in San Francisco, that she intended to outclass all other Blues singers in the country. Janis craved perfection; she wanted to be the best. Earlier, when she found an artist whose work she admired more than her own, she'd quit the art program at U.T. So much lay at stake.

Chet's friend, Travis Rivers arrived to accompany Janis to the West Coast. During the trip with Travis and a car full of hippies,*she scribbled a letter to an old friend. In letters Janis would often write "(moan)" or "(sigh)" to aid her correspondent in the reading of her true feelings. In this one she wrote "(moan)," described the churning of her stomach and, "Whew, I'm scared to death." [5]

Janis settled in San Francisco's Haight/Ashbury, the destination for migrating bohemians and young, aspiring hippies. She shopped thrift stores for any fabrics she could use

---

* While beatniks had dressed somberly and had been mostly apolitical, some of them joined the colorfully dressed counter-culture hippies as war protesters and advocates of civil rights.

for stage outfits and visited a dermatologist for her acne. She strung long lengths of bright beads to jazz up her costumes and to keep herself occupied.

She performed with Big Brother and the Holding Company: Peter Albin on bass, James Gurley and Sam Andrews on guitar and Dave Getz playing drums. They strummed and drummed loudly. Aiming to be heard, Janis screamed out her lyrics until the band learned to tone down. Her steely voice and physical sensuality seduced the audience with "Piece of My Heart" and "Summertime" and songs she wrote herself: "Women is Losers" and with Sam Andrews, "Call on Me." Her act, all sound and soul, raised the rafters of performance halls, creating something of a seismic sensation in the blues-rock arena.

The group took the spotlight twice at the Monterey Folk Fest in 1967. Audiences adored her and this was the pivotal point of Janis's career. Albert Grossman (Bob Dylan's manager) attended the festival looking for talent and said he wanted to manage Janis and the band. There were other opportunities as well, but Janis had befriended Linda Gravenites, her costume designer. She trusted Linda, who told her if she really wanted to be a star to sign with Grossman. Janis took the advice.

At age 24, she enjoyed the best year of her life with rehearsals, performances, and Linda Gravenites as roommate in San Francisco. Linda provided a quiet, stabilizing influence on Janis, who draped her bedroom in velvet and lace. The place was also home to George the Collie, and Sam the cat. Janis adored her pets.

In the summer of 1967, Janis wrote to her mother enclosing clippings from the San Francisco Chronicle and Examiner, explaining the attention the band had received since the Monterrey Music Festival. She expressed delight over articles in Newsweek and Time and told her mother to watch for the ABC Special about the festival. She described her new kitten, who along with George, had become part of her "strange family."

In January of 1968, Janis wrote the family to thank them for her birthday presents, saying that she never thought she would survive to age 25, "a quarter of a century." She explained why she had time to write; she had been ill and had to cancel three shows at the Fillmore, losing $8000, but feeling "nice and calm" after all the rest and recuperation. She advised them of her upcoming February/April tour to Philadelphia, Boston, New York, Toledo, and Detroit, in addition to performances at a few colleges.

When Janis and the band arrived in New York to rehearse for their grand introduction, they stayed at the Chelsea Hotel, a well-known literary hotel that Janis loved. (Dylan Thomas had lived and died there.) By the time of the national launch of Big Brother, Janis had perfected her style. Her debut at the Anderson[*] Theater in New York on February 17, 1968, was spectacular—a tour de force. She captivated the audience and caught the attention of critics who loved her costumes, her camaraderie with the crowd and her outsized voice, from loud and steely to soft and sweet.

Janis began something of a flirtation with the press. In lively interviews she offered conspicuous tidbits of her counter culture philosophy. She consistently gave reporters something to write about. "You gotta be true to yourself, because your self is all you really got in life," [6] she declared, or "I'm on an audience trip… I need them and they need me." [7]

Gifted intellectually and artistically but fragile emotionally, an appreciative audience could soothe her only temporarily. Offstage she felt an enduring loneliness.

Drinking whiskey slashed whatever impulse control she possessed. She'd been sober in Beaumont with the help of her family and a therapist but back in the rock-music milieu, she

---

[*] The Anderson, on the lower East side, had once seen performances of old Yiddish plays but for Janis it became a "rock hall." A month after Janis' debut with Big Brother, The Anderson closed, yielding to the new Fillmore East a few blocks away.

unleashed her emotions and gave in to temptations. Her flamboyant stage exhibitions spilled over into her personal life. Outfits, including boas, bangles and beads gave her an outcast, deranged look off stage. On the road, motel managers sometimes turned her away. "F--- you," she would say. She lived for fame and for the pleasure of the moment with Southern Comfort whiskey, her favorite companion. She bought a used Porsche and had the faces of Big Bother painted on a fender and a bloodied American flag on the trunk.*

Janis got the rave reviews–not Big Brother, and from the beginning of her new success the band quibbled. Eager to sustain her fame, she worked harder than the others. Nevertheless, band members felt bitter when she didn't share the credit.

Before they split up they recorded *Cheap Thrills.* From that album in 1968, "Piece of My Heart," was a number 12 hit. Big Brother had been her family. They'd lived together in one house and practiced and performed together for months. Wanting a change but not willing to break ties completely, she took guitarist Sam Andrew with her when she left; and Sam helped her transition to a new group.

She formed a corporation–"Fantality"(for fantasy and reality,)–appropriately dubbed since she apparently couldn't separate her stage self from her real self. Once on a New York street corner, dressed in her gypsy bracelets and boas, Janis encountered a bona fide clown, he with his Pagliacci eyes and wide mouth, red nose and baggy clothes. They stood in the street–the two of them–pointed at one another, and laughed and laughed.

---

* Janis' psychedelic Porsche can be viewed today at the Museum of the Gulf Coast in Port Arthur, Texas, where a section of the museum is dedicated to Janis Joplin.

It wasn't easy for Janis to get comfortable in her role as leader of Kosmic Blues, the new band. After two months of rehearsals, Janis bombed in Memphis* to her profound shame. But with time and work they improved. They toured Europe in April 1969 to packed concert halls. In London Janis had the spectators up, out of their seats dancing with the music. In Frankfurt she told the crowd, packed with U.S. soldiers,

"In the States, the only way to tell the good people is by their damn long hair. Over here, it seems to be the opposite." [8] She brought down the house. Janis had learned how to work an audience.

The words "Rebirth of the Blues" and a picture of Janis–ecstatically performing, holding a microphone, hair wild, and dress cut low–appeared on the cover of Newsweek on May 26 1969. In June, *I Got Dem Ol' Kosmic Blues Again, Mama!* was released by Columbia Records. Janis stayed off of drugs during the recording sessions but kept drinking. The Kozmic Blues recording got mixed reviews and went Gold.*

"Right now is where you are," [9] said Janis. On the road she had no choice. Stuck in a small hotel room in a strange city with only fellow workers for company and her gigs to focus on, living in the moment was obligatory. Despite her friendships with band members an empty feeling haunted her.

To escape and to stay occupied she read voraciously and thanked her father in letters home as well as in phone conversations for encouraging her to take literature seriously. Every time she changed residences she took along Billie Holiday's autobiography, *The Lady Sings the Blues.* She identified

---

* Memphis audiences heard the best black Blues musicians in the country. For Kosmic Blues they hardly applauded.

* A Gold record at that time required sales of 500,000 units, single or album. Now the criteria are different. Twice as many units must be sold to earn a Gold.

with Holiday who, like Janis, was a blues singer struggling to find peace.

Janis appeared at the Woodstock festival in August of 1969, where 500,000 Hippies showed up to get stoned, celebrate music and make a statement for peace.

The Joplin concerts, though emotionally and musically frenetic, were usually free of trouble and violence. At her concerts, people moved with the music, waved their bodies, and sang along. If Janis didn't see audience participation, she admonished them. "Feel," she demanded. "Why isn't there anyone dancing?" [10]

Janis cultivated her overtones to sound at times, like two voices singing in unison. But the gravelly component of her voice developed over years of drinking.

Her drug abuse worsened. Confronted by her manager Albert Grossman, and her friend and publicity agent Myra Friedman, she resolved to get clean. Albert put her in touch with a physician in New York, an expert in addiction, who gave her medicine to ease her off heroin.

The tragedy of her life was that she never took time from her hectic schedule to enter a long-term treatment program for her substance abuse problem. She didn't learn to stay away from drug-addicted boyfriends or from hotels where drugs were pushed. When she quit heroin, she didn't give up alcohol. The constant drinking set her up for relapses to narcotics. Except for her year at home in 1965, she was high on something almost all of her adult life.

Meanwhile, her earnings soared. Janis was frugal and she wanted to preserve funds in case her voice gave out or she decided to retire early. In December of 1969, she bought a modest home in Marin County north of San Francisco. Often a crowd gathered at her house and she picked up the tab for friends when they went to restaurants or bars. Friendship meant more to her than money, though she sometimes felt that her friends took advantage of her generosity.

Still she wished she had a partner. Married friends surrounded her, emphasizing her sense of solitude. She preferred a heterosexual lifestyle, having had several close, if brief, relationships with men; but if a proposal of marriage came up, her career stood in the way or conflicted with his, or the guy couldn't tolerate her lifestyle—at times wild, drunken and drug-crazed, or her affairs with women, (the longest with a drug addicted friend, Peggy Caserta.) Her long time housemate Linda Gravenites told her biographer, Myra Friedman, that Janis didn't love. "She needed." Janis sought pleasure peaks with drugs, alcohol and sex while a comfortable sense of self eluded her.

In February, Janis and Linda Gravenites took a vacation trip to Rio de Janerio for Carnival. Janis got off heroin and reportedly met a good man, David Niehaus, who fell in love with her. After the vacation they corresponded for a time and he came to visit her in California, but she couldn't leave the band; he didn't expect her to and he wouldn't give up his life to join her.

By the spring of 1970, she had been off drugs for months though she continued drinking tequila. She took time off from her racing, roaring touring schedule and studied music theory, took piano lessons and enjoyed her home in the woods. A new band, Full Tilt Boogie came together. Her friends helped her to find a nickname—Pearl—a pet name for her off-stage self.

* *In an April 1970 letter home, Janis told her parents about rehearsals with the new band and their great new songs. She apprised them of her lighter schedule—two months on tour and two months off, etc., and that she expected there would be time for a personal life. She described the expensive work she was having done on her house, the furniture and walls covered in fur and velvet, the colorful stained glass, the "eyeful of redwoods". She wrote to them about a new family member, an all white Great Pyrenees puppy, named Thurber.*

On May 29, 1970, Janis opened with the new band in Gainesville, Florida. Performances in Jacksonville and Miami followed. John Cooke* accompanied her on the road. After a gig in Baltimore they crossed the border into Canada, and now clean, she had nothing to hide from the customs agents according to Cooke.

She enjoyed her fame. She made several appearances on Dick Cavett's T.V. show and felt honored to be his guest. With beads, bracelets and hot pink feathers in her hair, she sang on his late night show June 25,1970, with the Full Tilt Boogie Band: John Till (guitar), Brad Campbell (bass), Richard Bell (piano), Ken Pearson (organ), Clark Pierson, (drums). They performed "Move Over," Janis's own composition, and "Get It While You Can," by J. Ragovoy** and M. Shuman. Janis talked amicably with the other guests: newscaster Chet Huntley and actors Raquel Welch and Douglas Fairbanks, Jr. She told Cavett she'd be going to her high school reunion and the audience laughed, knowing of her antipathy toward the Port Arthur hometown folk.

"Would you like to go, man?" [11] she asked Cavett.

"…I don't have that many friends in your high school class," Cavett joked.

"Neither do I," said Janis. "That's why I'm going." The audience giggled. "They laughed me out of class, out of town,

---

* For much of her career John Cooke arranged life on the road for Janis and the band. He'd been with Big Brother and continued for a time as "roadie" with Kosmic Blues. John was fond of Janis. He worked to make everything happen in an organized way: arranging airline tickets, limo rides, transportation of the instruments, and the logistics of the appearances in the performance halls.

** Jerry Ragovoy, who died in 2011 at the age of 80 had written or co-written other songs which became hits for Janis including, "Try (Just a Little Bit Harder)," and "Cry Baby."

out of the state," she said of her classmates, "so I'm going home." [12]

She took three friends with her to the reunion, including John Cooke, for moral support. But Janis didn't mend any fences, and classmates who had rejected her a decade earlier still withheld the love she craved.

That summer she'd returned to Austin for Threadgill's Jubilee Birthday party, traveling from Hawaii where she toured with the band. For the huge crowd she sang, "Me and Bobby McGee," written by Kris Kristofferson.

From the road that summer Janis phoned Dorothy Joplin. She said,

"Mother, I'm just so tired." [13] When Mrs. Joplin suggested she work less, Janis indicated she had to keep making money, not for herself but "for them." Despite her comments, Janis actually liked a busy schedule, sometimes saying that she lived to perform because only then did she feel alive.

Throughout her life in letters home to parents and siblings, Janis shared both her troubles and her successes. She sought the family's approval even while acknowledging her uniqueness, knowing that they might never understand her.

In August of 1970, the Full Tilt Boogie Band accompanied Janis to Los Angeles to make an album. They stayed at the Landmark Hotel, where Janis would read by the pool during free time and sometimes have a swim after work. The Landmark, a place frequented by drug pushers, was a poor choice of hotels for someone trying to stay clean.

Recording was tedious, with takes, retakes and hours of waiting to do the vocals while the band recorded their parts in layers, all to be integrated later.

Janis was at the top of her world. She clicked with the band. Paul Rothschild, the producer for the recording, became a friend. Paul helped Janis to impose the nuances of her voice on the music for a better sound. He and Janis planned future collaborations. Both Paul and Janis owned Porsches. They rode with the wind along the Los Angeles hillsides, one behind the other, convertible tops down and tearing around curves.

In mid-September, Jimi Hendrix died of an overdose of barbiturates. His death haunted Janis but she remarked to another friend that she didn't think two rock stars would "go out" in the same year.

Janis had promised to marry her then boyfriend Seth Morgan, whom she'd met when he delivered drugs to her door. She had doubts about him. She needed companionship and Seth was often absent—sometimes with other women. Friends suspected the union would never happen but on the last day of her life she had been on the phone to City Hall about the marriage license. She had tried to call Seth but couldn't reach him.

After being clean for several weeks, Janis had a couple of drinks and shot up with heroin by hypodermic—into the skin instead of a vein. The drug, four or five times stronger than usual, hadn't been tested. During the next half hour she breezed to the Landmark lobby to get change for the cigarette machine, bought smokes and had a conversation with the desk clerk. She got back to her room about the time the drug reached its maximum impact. Combined with the alcohol it devastated her. She reentered her room, threw her cigarette pack on the bedside table, and still clutching in her fist the change from the machine, fell over dead.*

Eighteen hours later when she was late for the recording studio, John Cooke got a key from the hotel desk to check her room. He found Janis wedged between the bed and the night table, cold and stiff.

Janis was 27 years old on October 4, 1970, when she died, according to the autopsy, of an accidental overdose.

---

* Others died that night from the same batch of heroin.

152

A private funeral service took place on October 7, and five days later her cremated remains were scattered along the pacific coastline.

The Album, *Pearl*, released after her death, was her biggest smash hit. "Me and Bobby McGee," from that album was her only number-one single. With that song she had returned, the way she'd begun, to her folk and country roots.

Janis was inducted into the Rock and Roll Hall of Fame in 1995, twenty-five years after her death.

In 2005, she was awarded, posthumously, The Grammy Lifetime Achievement Award, for her creative contributions of outstanding artistic significance to the field of recording.

The Sculpture of Janis Joplin, housed in the Museum of the Gulf Coast in Port Arthur, Texas, is by Doug Clark. Photo used with permission.

Janis Joplin:
Bibliography:

Amburn, Ellis. *Pearl: The Obsessions and Passions of Janis Joplin*: Warner Books, New York, NY: 1993.

Echols, Alice, *Scars of Sweet Paradise: The Life and Times of Janis Joplin*: Metropolitan Books of Henry Holt and Co, Inc. New York, NY: 1999.

Friedman, Myra. *Buried Alive: The Biography of Janis Joplin*, William Morrow and Co New York NY:1973

Friedman, Myra. *Buried Alive: The Biography of Janis Joplin*, Harmony Books of Crown Publishers. New York, NY: 1992.

Hilburn, Robert. *Cornflakes With John Lennon: and other tales from a rock 'n' roll life*, Rodale Inc. New York: 2009

Joplin, Laura. *Love, Janis*: Villard Books of Random House Inc. New York, NY: 1992.

La Blanc, Michael L Editor. *Contemporary Musicians Volume III*: 127-128, Janis Joplin, Singer, Songwriter.

Newsweek Magazine, May 26, 1969, Cover

Rolling Stone Magazine Web Site

Whitburn, Joel's Top Pop, Singles 1955-1993 Billboard, Record Research Inc. Menomonee Falls, Wisconsin: 1994

The Letters:

Excerpts, in italics, from some of Janis's letters home are paraphrased from the book, *Love Janis*, written by her sister, Laura Joplin.

Quotes:

1 "Man, I'd rather..." *Buried Alive* – Page 136, Friedman, 1992

2 "Then the whole world..." *Buried Alive* – Page 12, Friedman, 1992

3 "I was treated..." *The Obsessions and Passions of Janis Joplin*, Page 30, Amburn

4 "the greatest white..." *The Obsessions and Passions of Janis Joplin*, Page 61, Amburn

5 "Whew, I am scared..." *Buried Alive* – Page 70, Friedman, 1992

6 "You gotta be..." *Love, Janis: The songs, The Letters, The Soul of Janis Joplin* – from the liner notes

7 "I'm on an audience..." *Love, Janis* – Page 216, Laura Joplin

8 "In the states..." *Scars of Sweet Paradise* – Page 247, Echols

9 "Right now is..." *Buried Alive* – Page 154, Friedman, 1992

10 "Feel, "Why aren't you..." *Buried Alive* – Page 170, Friedman, 1992

11&12 "Would you like to..." - Video, The Rock Icons, The Dick Cavett Show

13 "Mother, I'm just..." *Buried Alive* – Page 234, Friedman, 1992

More Notes – Janis Joplin

Page 137 - Weighing 5 ½ pounds – Page 28 – *Love, Janis* – Laura Joplin, hereafter referred to as Joplin

The children, Mrs Joplin said, were encouraged –Page 12 – *Buried Alive, The Biography of Janis Joplin*, Myra Friedman, 1992: hereafter referred to as Friedman

Page 138 - appearance and "terrible skin condition" – Page 16 – Friedman

They climbed the water towers – Page 17 – Friedman

The police escorted Janis to the bus – Page 80 – Joplin

Seth was kind of in the background... – Page 11 – *Scars of Sweet Paradise The Life and Times of Janis Joplin* – Echols, Alice

Father /daughter conversations on the porch – Joplin

Page 139 - Mother's two sisters – Page 92 – Joplin

She soon got a job – Page 93 – ibid

Janis moved into the low rent – Page 96 – Joplin

She enrolled as a student – Page 98 – Joplin

Janis persuaded them to let her enroll – Page 106 – Joplin

Discography:

Cheap Thrills, Big Brother and the Holding Company, 1999 Sony Music Entertainment Inc./originally recorded and released, 1968/ Manufactured by Columbia Records New York, NY, and Legacy. Re-mastered, 1999
The Songs, The Letters, The Soul of Janis Joplin: Sony Music Entertainment, Columbia and Legacy, 2001.
Pearl – Sony Music Entertainment, Inc. Originally recorded 1970, and released, 1971/Manufactured by Columbia Records New York, NY Re-mastered, 1999

Videography:

The Monterey International Pop Festival: 2007 Razor &Tie Ltd. New York, N.Y.
The Rock Icons: The Dick Cavett Show, Daphne Productions, Sony, Los Angeles: 2005

The photograph of the Janis Joplin Sculpture by Douglas Clark is courtesy of the Museum of the Gulf Coast, Port Arthur, Texas.

Selena in performance, (Larry Busacca/Retna Ltd./Corbis)

Selena   (1971 – 1995)

She was born on Easter Sunday, April 16, 1971, in Lake Jackson, Texas, weighing five pounds and ten and one-half ounces. Her parents, Marcella and Abraham Quintanilla, who expected a boy, had chosen the name Marc Anthony. Marcella's hospital roommate had selected Selena–a girl's name–not suitable for her own baby son. The Quintanillas liked the sound of "Sa-Lee-na," with the Anglo pronunciation, and took it for their tiny daughter.

The Quintanillas are Mexican-Americans whose forebears had occupied that Southeast corner of Texas for a century or more. Abraham loved music and played guitar in a band before the demands of a family led him to seek and find work at Dow Chemical Company. When his children were old enough, he began to instruct them on musical instruments while indulging his own passion.

By the time Selena was five, her older siblings, A.B. (Abraham III), thirteen, played bass while nine-year-old Suzette played drums under Abraham's guidance in their soundproof garage. Selena begged her father to allow her to sing with the family band. When Selena began singing with them, Abraham taught her a few Spanish songs phonetically so that they could perform Tejano, the popular local music.

Tejano music grew from the roots of the first Texas settlers, who came with their accordions from Germany and Eastern Europe. Adding 12-string guitars, imported from Northern Mexico, plus drums, and bass, they played "happy music" that one could dance to, often polkas. When the big bands of Benny Goodman and Glen Miller rose to fame, they influenced the Tex/Mex "conjunto" sound. (Conjunto connotes the bringing together of people and instruments to produce the celebratory music now called Tejano, in which an accordion drones the essential sound.)

Tejano songs reflect the dual cultures of people living between the Rio Grande and Nueces Rivers where Corpus

Christi sits at the geographical core. When Selena was born most of the listeners to Tejano lived within these confines. Over the course of her lifetime, due to the popularity and proliferation of the music of Selena y Los Dinos and other contemporary groups through performance and radio, Tejano music broke through those borders, reaching all Spanish speaking countries and cultures, including all parts of the USA where Spanish is spoken.

In her grammar school years, Selena was bubbly and energetic—she roller-skated, jumped rope, and played with dolls. Her family called her "Preciosa." At school she worked diligently and quietly, made good grades, and played happily with her friends at recess. Teachers and classmates liked her.

His parents were members of Jehovah's Witnesses, but Abraham's family didn't officially join the congregation. Perhaps their musical activities conflicted with some of the church's tenets. They did consider themselves followers of the faith, however. Due to Jehovah's Witnesses' beliefs, Selena withdrew from certain schoolroom parties, either going home or to the library. Selena didn't seem to be bothered much by the conditions of her faith. On one occasion, she arrived at school on her birthday and told the class they weren't allowed to sing to her, but they sang "Happy Birthday," anyway.

In the summer of 1981, when she was ten years old, Selena's voice resonated with new depth and her father noticed a sparkle in her stage presence. Abraham and his partners opened a restaurant in Lake Jackson—Papa Gayo's—offering Mexican food and entertainment, and providing the family band, "Southern Pearl and Selena and Company," a place to perform.

One year later, when the oil market crashed and the Texas economy slumped, the restaurant went broke and the Quintanillas lost their house. They struggled through hard times. Abraham had given up his job at Dow Chemical Company to follow his musical quest. For a few weeks, Selena lived with a relative while Abraham reestablished himself financially. Eventually he moved the family to Corpus Christi and went to work for his brother's truck rental business.

Selena later said that the move to Corpus Christi in 1983 marked the real beginning of their musical careers. Always, she remembered fondly the green grass and lush trees of Lake Jackson, riding her bike there, playing hide and seek with neighborhood children, and eating out at Sonic, a drive-in restaurant, and at Dairy Queen.

More Latinos than Anglos lived in Corpus Christi, the center of what was called "la Onda,"–"the wave." The Tejano music wave dominated radio airtime.*

The first Tejano record to exceed 100,000 sales was "Te Traigo Estas Flores," sung by Freddie Martinez. Written by Joe Mejía and recorded in 1972 when Selena was a year old, it got lots of jukebox time. Martinez had grown up with polkas, rancheras (Mexican blues), and cumbias (dance tunes). He added a mix of mambo and cha-cha to the traditional sound.

Tejano songs sometimes contained both Spanish and English lyrics, at times lamenting lost love. But usually the music resonated with joy and almost always it provided a dancehall beat. "La Onda" boosted pride in local culture and heritage. In 1979, when Selena was eight, an annual Tejano Music Awards ceremony was initiated.

Abraham opted to stay within the Tejano music culture to please local audiences. When he was young, his mentor, Johnny Herrera, had told him, "You've got to get into the Mexican market. You're never going to compete with the

---

* Station KCCT–AM played Chicano and Tejano music in preference to Mariachi and Spanish music. Several radio announcers flipped back and forth between the English and Spanish languages and listeners became accustomed to this free wheeling style of broadcasting. A full-time Spanish T.V. station entertained the citizenry. In Corpus Christi, a Mexican/American had won a seat in the state senate.

'Four Aces.'"[1] It was good advice. Singing Tejano music, his group had enjoyed frequent gigs and more than a little fame.

Abraham knew his way around the Corpus music world. His own, earlier teenage combo had been called Los Dinos (The Boys), a familiar title. When the family band took their new name, Selena y Los Dinos, they got work more easily.

Until she began singing with the band, Selena knew only English. Abraham painstakingly taught Selena the Tejano songs. He would sing duets with her or accompany her on guitar. The band played weddings, birthdays, and road shows, barely scratching out a living. Early on, their performances included some audible musical mistakes. Featuring Selena, a female singer, in a male-dominated culture provided another challenge. Through it all, Abraham encouraged the others. They worked hard and improved year-after year.

"There were a lot of disappointing times," [2] said Selena later in an interview. She recalled performances when audiences were small and the pay was minimal. The other band members had to be paid before the family got their share. But whenever they wanted to give up and get regular jobs, an encouraging incident boosted their spirits.

"Something always just held us to the music,"[3] said Selena. "If we got five or ten dollars, my God...We were all happy," [4]

In 1985, two Corpus Christi teens came to work with the band: Rocky Garcia on guitar and Ricky Vela on keyboard. The modern keyboard could replicate the hum of the accordion, so basic to the Tejano sound.

Selena y Los Dinos recorded "Oh, Mama" for Cara Records and got some radio play with it. They appeared on the Johnny Canales Show, the number one television program for Latin American acts of that era. Canales saw the promise of success in Selena and invited her, regularly, to appear on his TV extravaganza. He teased Selena about her spoken Spanish, which was limited, though she sang like a native.

Due to economic demands, the dropout rate from school was significantly higher for Mexican-American children. Selena frequently missed classes on Fridays and Mondays when she traveled with the band. She made good grades but some of the teachers criticized her parents for taking her out of school so much. In her eighth grade year, Selena's parents removed her from public education. She did homework on the road and on days off until, eventually, she earned her high school diploma through the mail from The American School of Chicago.

As to the band, Abraham managed them and booked the gigs. Brother A.B. played bass guitar and produced their music. Sister Suzette drummed and did publicity. Marcella also traveled with the band and helped with staging and lighting. They worked as a team, Selena later explained. Everyone had a job and they supported one another's talents for the good of all.

Of her mother, Selena said, "She is loving, sentimental, honest, uncomplicated. My Mom is everything that is good. I want to be like her." 5

Abraham was tougher. His voice and demeanor were sometimes gruff, but he loved his wife and children and had their welfare at heart. He maintained a position of authority

---

· Cara Records, run by Bob Gréver, was an important label for Tejano music. Gréver's contract producer, Manny Guerra, was the best in the business, and together they recorded the well known Gruppa Maz and La Mafia.

both within the family and in his business dealings. As the success of Los Dinos increased and the group expanded, Abraham quit working on stage. He had enough to do with booking and managing the performances.

Over time, Tejano music would evolve to include elements of rhythm & blues, pop, folk, salsa*and Colombian dance music. Selena and A.B. incorporated these various elements into their music. Their music would always change and grow with the musicians adding their own nuances to the Los Dinos sound. Meanwhile, Selena's voice grew richer as she matured and experience became her teacher.

In 1986, "Dame Un Beso" was nominated at the Tejano Music Awards as Song of the Year and Single of the Year. "A Million to One," sung in English, was the first number one record for Selena y Los Dinos. In 1987 and 1988, the Tejano Music Awards honored her with "Female Entertainer of the Year." Selena had become a regional teenaged star.

By 1987, Selena y Los Dinos played large venues, some in Houston, opening for famous Tejano groups such as Mazz and La Mafia. Sophisticated light and sound systems and glittering costumes magnified the professional atmosphere of their shows.

For two years in a row Selena had won awards, and the group could now command higher fees. They traded-in the van and trailer for a bus they named "Big Bertha."

Within "Big Bertha" they traveled, slept and ate. Once, Johnny Canales visited her after a performance as a tired Selena sat on one of the seats in "Big Bertha" eating her late dinner of beans and franks from a can. Canales asked her,

"Selena, are you still eating that stuff?"

---

* Salsa, a genre of music deriving from Cuban Son and Mambo, is essentially the pulse of Cuban dance music. The terms Latin jazz and Salsa are sometimes used interchangeably.

"I don't want to get too used to the good life,"[6] she answered. Canales assured her that one day she would be eating nothing but steak.

The bus offered little warmth in winter and, in summer, no cooling other than that which came through open windows. But it provided respite from the numerous dancehall performances. Riding over Texas prairies between gigs, Selena did schoolwork. She sketched designs for the band's costumes, made belts and sewed sequins and sparkles onto her stage outfits. She played jokes on the other troubadours. Selena always remembered the hours aboard "Big Bertha" with a smile.

In 1988, The Manny Guerra RP Label released two albums by Selena y Los Dinos: *Preciosa* and *Dulce Amor*. Of the 10 or 15 radio stations playing Tejano music, a Billboard poll listed Selena as the artist most frequently selected.

By 1989, Selena was well known across the Lone Star state. At age 18, she signed a contract with Coca Cola to be their spokesperson for Latin markets. For Coca Cola, the young singer had a clean, strong, healthy image. With her black hair, dark eyes, and engaging smile, she was lovely to look at. People liked her effervescent personality. She earned $145,000 a year as the Coca Cola girl, and Selena's ads reached all of the Texas population as well as every sector of the country where large numbers of Latin Americans lived.

Her first Capitol Record album, *Selena*, included a mixture of Tejano and Latin pop songs. "Contigo Quiero Estar," made it to number eight on the Billboard Mexican Regional chart. As earnings increased, the band bought new equipment and road gear.

They grew. Singer Pete Astudillo came aboard to harmonize with Selena and to help A.B. write Spanish lyrics. Joe Ortega joined the group as a second keyboardist.

In 1989, A.B. attended a rehearsal of the Shelly Lares (Tejano) band to hear Chris Perez, a guitarist. Awed by Chris's strong lyric style, A.B. offered him a job right then with Selena y Los Dinos. After thinking about it for a day or two and consulting with his current band, Chris accepted. Chris already knew the work of Selena y Los Dinos and loved their music. He admired A.B.'s talents and wanted to be a part of this innovative group. For several years Selena and Chris's relationship remained a professional one.

In 1990, Selena won Female Vocalist of the Year and Female Entertainer of the Year at the Tejano Music Awards. She planned to cross over into the Latin international market.

A.B. had become a fine arranger and record producer. He and Pete Astrudillo wrote many of the songs for their next album, *Ven Con Migo*. The album reached the top of the Mexican charts for Billboard and stayed there for 56 weeks. "Baila Esta Cumbia" climbed to number eight in the singles regionals. Selena had become one of the top four Tejano music acts with Mazz and La Mafia, and Emilio Navaira. Also a Coca Cola spokesperson, Emilio Navaira sometimes sang duets with Selena.

On the Johnny Canales show in 1991, Selena y Los Dinos appeared in outfits she designed: black and white cowhide costumes for the band and slim trousers, a Madonna style bustier and white boots for herself. She danced and sang "Baila Esta Cumbia," working the entire stage with her seismic performance. "Selenamania" erupted among the fans.

Success overwhelmed the band. They shuffled schedules, made recordings, performed and traveled. The Quintanillas didn't have time to organize the fans. For months, Yolanda Saldivar, a Registered Nurse, had been asking family members if she could run Selena's fan club. Finally, Abraham gave the okay for Yolanda to take charge. Starting in late 1991, and over the next several years under Yolanda's supervision, the fan

166

club expanded to over 4,000 members. Selena was grateful and she and Yolanda became friends.

Selena's social life was centered within her own family, the band, and the few fans and friends that Abraham invited backstage. She retained a certain innocence and naiveté due to this sheltering. And, not surprisingly, the man she married was already a member of their musical team.

Selena and Chris Perez first became aware of a romantic interest in one another during an Acapulco vacation with the band and a rare opportunity to relax and have fun. They sat side-by-side on the airplane trip home. Selena took Chris's hand during some turbulence and from that day they stole private moments together while hiding their meetings from her father. Within a few months Abraham discovered their relationship and after an explosion of temper, fired Chris from the band.

Though Chris left Selena y Los Dinos and hired on with another band, the couple struggled to find time to see each other while avoiding Abraham's wrath. Chris introduced Selena to his parents. The young couple visited there regularly and Selena became close to Chris's family.

After several weeks of clandestine meetings, Selena knocked loudly on the door of Chris's Corpus Christi hotel room and announced that she wanted to marry him right now, today. In Selena's mind this would be the only way in which Abraham would be forced to accept them as a couple.

Though she had always imagined an elaborate wedding, Selena and Chris married quietly at the courthouse on April 2, 1992. Sure enough, Abraham softened; he hugged Chris and took him into the family. Within a few months, the newly weds moved into a house in Corpus Christi next door to Marcella and Abraham. A.B. and family shared a house on the other side of their parents. After Suzette married, she and her husband lived just a few blocks away.

Fans saw Selena and Chris as a perfect couple. She was talkative and vivacious. He was quiet and shy. She didn't cook often, because of their busy travel calendar. They appeared at local restaurants for dinner always holding hands. She took his name and became Selena Quintanilla-Perez.

Selena liked beans and sausage as well as double pepperoni, thin-crusted pizza. At home the couple had His and Hers tortilla chip bags so one couldn't accuse the other of eating all the chips.

Selena wanted five children but Chris thought two would be plenty for a couple as busy with road tours as they were. They agreed to postpone the discussion until their schedule allowed them to consider expanding the family.

A lover of animals, Selena coaxed Chris into buying a black Pomeranian puppy. They named her Pebbles. Soon they added a blue-eyed miniature Doberman called Jax, an abbreviated moniker of Chris's Jackson guitar. A Husky and two Mastiffs later joined the family. When one of the pets wandered away and neighborhood children helped to bring it home, Selena rewarded the kids with Selena T-shirts and McDonald's meals. Neighbors would sometimes see the singer playing with her dogs in her yard, washing her car in the driveway, or mowing her grass or that of her parents, next door.

Selena's charm and talent made her an excellent musical collaborator. She exuded energy and everyone who knew her wanted to work with her. At the 1992 Tejano Music Awards she sang a duet with Alvaro Torres, a Honduran with fans throughout Central America and Puerto Rico. The success of their single "Buenos Amigos," gained her new fans, widening her popularity.

For the next album, *Entre a Mi Mundo*, every song was written "in-house," usually with her brother, A.B., writing music for lyrics written by Pedro Astudillo or Ricky Vela. "Amame" on that album was a Selena/Astudillo creation. Selena helped to create the lyrical content of the songs composed for her voice. She sang her dreams of the life she imagined she would have had if she had stayed in school as a teen, dressed up for peers, and had boyfriends and dates.

Selena celebrated the Barbie doll image she admired. She selected this imagery for the costumes she designed for herself and the band. She appeared on the cover of *Entre a Mi Mundo* in a self-designed black and white outfit. The album remained on the Latino top 50 charts for over a year and earned #1 Regional Mexican Album of the year. On the inside cover following the credits there is written: *Selena y Los Dinos – Club De Admiradores – Yolanda Saldivar – Presidente.*

Selena was now becoming the biggest Tejano act in Mexico. She had conquered the Latin market. During a press tour in Mexico, one reporter called her "una artista del pueblo," an artist of the people. Selena hugged all the reporters so that no one would write a disparaging comment about her Spanish. And no one did. But she was determined to speak like the locals, and she traveled to Mexico City and Monterrey for several extended visits for the purpose of perfecting her Spanish.

On February 7, 1993, Selena y Los Dinos opened to a sold out house at Memorial Coliseum in Corpus Christi. The album from that hometown concert, *Selena Live*, her fourth for EMI Latin, generated high record sales and earned a Grammy.

At the Tejano Music Awards in 1993, she won again: Female Singer of the Year and Female Entertainer of the Year.

Meanwhile, Tejano music mushroomed. Selena and the band played large houses, including the Alamo Dome and the Astrodome. They entertained eager audiences in Monterrey, Mexico. All-Tejano radio stations took root in San Antonio and Dallas, and San Antonio became for Tejano music what Nashville was for "country."

Selena didn't intend to abandon her Tejano fans. But now that the band had successfully crossed over into the Latin International market, they planned an English album. In 1993,

Selena y los Dinos signed with SBK Records for the English language record.

Satisfied with their professional and financial successes, Abraham had been in no rush to cross over. "Take a look around..." [7] he said. "We're doing fine." The clubs where the band performed were packed with fans. "Big Bertha" had been replaced with three elegant vans. Q Productions, their new state-of-the-art recording studio in Corpus Christi, provided all the electronics needed to make world-class recordings. And Q-Productions included a sewing and fashion wing for Selena's apparel merchandise.

Selena had long been interested in fashion design, and wanted a shop where she could sell her clothes. But because of her performance schedule she couldn't devote herself fulltime to the enterprise. Fortunately, designer Martin Gomez liked her ideas, and his expertise made it possible for Selena to enter the retail fashion world. Always supportive of her dreams and ambitions, Chris Perez helped his wife find a shop for her wares and provided some hands-on carpentry to get it ready for business.

In January 1994, Selena's biggest dream came true when "Selena, Etc. Salon and Boutique" opened in Corpus Christi. Eight months later a second "Selena, Etc." opened in San Antonio. Her labels read "Designed by Martin Gomez Exclusively for Selena." Fashion design had been her hobby. Now it became her business. In music her father ran the show but in the boutiques, Selena ruled.

Selena invited Yolanda Saldivar to manage the clothing boutiques and presented her with company credit cards. Martin Gomez made it clear from the outset that he didn't like Yolanda. She had taken over his desk without asking, interfered with operations of the boutiques, irritated staff members, and fired anyone she didn't like. Over time, Selena's father learned that Yolanda's fan club duties had begun to falter. An employee, on an errand to Yolanda's house, found a shrine to Selena there with pictures of Selena all over the walls, an uncommon collection for a mature woman to display. As time went by Yolanda saw herself increasingly as her employer's protector. She tried to create barriers between Selena and her fans, and between Selena and her family.

Selena hadn't known when she hired her that Yolanda had been accused of stealing from a prior employer. When Yolanda volunteered as the fan club president, the family trusted in her honesty. Since Selena's touring schedule left her with little time to take care of the details of the businesses, she depended on Yolanda. If anyone complained, Selena defended her friend.

Selena was happy singing on the road. On days off she liked going to her boutique in Corpus Christi for a manicure, facial and hair styling. She enjoyed going to the salon in street clothes so that other customers didn't recognize her as she listened to comments from the patrons. Her family teased her, saying that she only wanted to own the boutiques so that she could be pampered for two or three hours for free.

She and Chris bought Porsches, hers a black 968, and his a red Targa. Selena loved to drive and admired Chris's car because of the crimson color and because it would go faster. Chris eventually gave it to her. He wanted a truck so that he could haul his instruments around, and so that they could take their dogs along on pleasure trips.

For their first wedding anniversary, Selena surprised Chris with a Chevy Silverado truck, which Chris had admired. Chris bought a motorcycle, which Selena insisted on learning to drive, though Chris feared for her safety.

They listened to her favorite cassettes—Whitney Houston, Janet Jackson and Bonnie Raitt—when a measure of freedom appeared.

Chris often gave Selena bouquets of the long-stemmed white roses she liked. Each time, she received them with the same enthusiasm and kind appreciation that she held from her humble beginnings.

Chris gave her the first of her Fabergé eggs after she admired one in a hotel gift shop. Selena collected thirty or forty of the ceramic creations as a celebration of new life, and perhaps her own Easter birthday.

Knowing of Selena's fascination with these works of art, Yolanda hired a jeweler to fashion a finger ring of white gold and diamonds forming an egg shape, and paid for it with her Selena Design House credit card. Though she had solicited donations from employees for the gift, she presented the valuable ring to Selena as if Yolanda were the only contributor. Selena loved her present and had no idea that her employees chipped in to buy it.

February 1994, found Selena at the Houston Livestock Show and Rodeo, where she performed at the Astrodome for the rodeo for the second consecutive year.* Two days later she was in New York with Chris, at Radio City Music Hall in a stunning white gown, attending the Grammys. The *Selena Live* album had been nominated for a Grammy for Best Mexican/American Album, which she won that evening. She performed at the 1994 Tejano Music Awards in March and won Female Vocalist of the Year, Female Entertainer of the Year, Best International Artist, and Album of the Year.

Selena's fifth album for EMI Latin–*Amor Prohibido*–came out in April. In it she sang for the Spanish International market: "Techno Cumbia," "Amor Prohibido," "Bidi Bidi Bom Bom,"**which she wrote herself with improvisational input

---

* In 1995, Selena would appear again at the Live Stock Show and Rodeo in the Astrodome, and give a memorable performance of "Fotos y Recuerdos."

** "Amor Prohibido" is translated as "Forbidden Love." "Techno Cumbia," is a dance song with a beat, and rap-like lyrics. "Bidi Bidi Bom Bom" is the onomatopoeic palpitation of a young girl's heart when her favorite boyfriend comes near.

from the band, and a remake of "Fotos y Recuerdos" from The Pretenders, with lyrics by Ricky Vela. Half of the music on this album was experimental. Most of the songs were cumbias (dance songs). The album soared to the top of Billboard's Latin Top-50 album charts. It went quadruple platinum, selling 400,000 copies.

In May, Selena won an award in Miami at the Billboard Latin Music Awards. The September issue of *Texas Monthly Magazine* listed her as one of the twenty most influential Texans for 1994. Coca Cola bottled 8-ounce commemorative drink containers with Selena's signature in limited edition. The labels read, "Cinco años contigo...Siempre Selena, Siempre Coca Cola." "Five years with you...Always Selena, Always Coca Cola."

On stage Selena wore spangled bustiers and skin-tight pants. Off stage she became the model girl-next-door. She visited schools where she admonished the students, "Don't drink. Don't take drugs. Remain chaste. Stay in school." Students admired and emulated her.

In his 2012 book, *To Selena With Love*, Chris tells of only one "rough patch," in their married life, born of total exhaustion from their travel and performance lives. There weren't many breaks, not enough sleep, and tempers were short. The acrimony was brief and never recurred. When they renewed their love for each other, they wanted privacy from fans and family.

They bought a ten-acre lot in Corpus Christi. After the English album was finished and their professional futures better secured, the couple wanted to start a family. They happily visited the property where they planned to build a house and raise children. Selena had often admired Chris's spontaneous and playful way with kids and could easily imagine him as father to their own.

In 1995, Selena took many of the Tejano Music Awards, but while her music career flourished, the fashion business floundered. She wanted to rescue the enterprise by expanding into the broader Mexican markets. Now a well-known star in Monterrey, Selena anticipated huge sales to its affluent citizens. Meanwhile, her employees notified Abraham that Yolanda was stealing from the business.

At a family meeting with Yolanda present, the Quintanilla's–Selena, Abraham, A.B. and Suzette–confronted Yolanda. When asked about the missing monies, all she could manage to say was, "I don't know. I don't know."

Abraham barred her from Q Productions and Suzette called her a thief. Yolanda's name was removed from company checks and she lost check-signing authority for the boutiques. But tragically, Selena didn't fire her that day.

The following day Yolanda appeared at "A Place to Shoot," a gun shop near San Antonio, where she purchased a .38 caliber revolver. She told the owners that she worked as a home health nurse and that a patient's family member had threatened her. She picked up the gun on March 13, after the routine background check.

Selena, in her quest to get bank records from Yolanda before she fired her, told her that they were still friends and that Yolanda could help her expand the business to Mexico. Yolanda showed Selena the gun she'd bought, "for protection." Selena told Yolanda she should return it. On March 15, Yolanda took the gun back to the store, telling the shopkeepers that she would borrow her father's gun instead.

After a heated meeting with Selena, in which Yolanda failed to provide the bank statements, Yolanda returned to the gun shop, repurchased the revolver and drove with her sister to Monterrey, ostensibly to develop plans for the boutique. When a suspicious bank teller notified Selena that Yolanda tried to clean out an account, Selena called Yolanda to ask her to bring the financial records for the boutiques to Corpus Christi so that tax preparation could begin.

Thursday, March 30, was a beautiful spring day in Corpus Christi. Selena stopped to buy shoes and some in-line skates anticipating a trip to California where she would do a concert and perhaps have time to skate in the sunshine. In spite of a full schedule for the following week, she called her Mother and took her to lunch. Marcella had injured her ankle in an accident and her foot was swollen, but she wanted to see her daughter. They enjoyed a four-hour lunch at Olive Garden, sharing stories and memories. On the way home Selena was singing while driving and her mother leaned over and told Selena that she loved her.

"I love you, too, Mama,"[8] replied Selena.

Selena stopped at her boutique for a few hours of pampering, after which she went home, where Chris's father was expected to visit for a few days.

Returning from Mexico, Yolanda had driven her sister home to San Antonio, and called Selena to say she'd arrived at the Day's Inn on Navigation Boulevard in Corpus Christi. Late in the evening, Selena and Chris drove to the Day's Inn. Yolanda had said she wanted to see Selena alone, so Chris stayed in his truck while Selena went inside to get the statements. Yolanda told Selena she had been raped and revealed some torn clothing. Selena volunteered to take her to the hospital but she didn't want to go.

When Selena didn't return right away, Chris went to check on her. He found two unhappy looking females in room 158, but no trouble. Back at home, Selena and Chris sat down to pay bills, visit with Chris's father and plan the next day's meal, Chris's favorite, marinated black-tipped shark. Selena had noticed that the bank records Yolanda had given her were incomplete and now her cell phone rang. It was Yolanda. She told Selena she had found the missing papers and asked her to return to the motel, but Chris persuaded Selena to wait until morning to deal with Yolanda. Neither Chris nor Selena believed Yolanda's bizarre rape story. It was another of her stalling tactics.

Selena admitted to Chris that she now knew she could no longer trust Yolanda. Chris thought of her as a misfit who used Selena's friendship to increase her own feelings of power. But no one considered Yolanda dangerous.

When Selena awoke the next morning, she showered quietly and dressed in green work out clothes. She had forgotten that Chris's father was in the house and when she stepped into the hallway, he appeared suddenly through the guest room doorway. Selena screamed, waking Chris. She recovered instantly and laughingly told Chris everything was fine and to go back to sleep.

She took Chris's truck because she couldn't find the keys to her car. His cell phone was inside. She drove to the motel, knocked on door 158, and accompanied Yolanda to the hospital. The results of the exam were inconclusive.

During the return trip with Yolanda to the motel, Selena called Chris from his cell phone to explain why she took his truck and to say she'd be home soon. That was the last conversation Chris would have with his beloved wife.

When they reached Yolanda's room, Selena placed the paperwork on the bed and began to remove the gemstone ring that Yolanda had given her. When she saw that Yolanda had a gun, she turned to run. A shot hit Selena's shoulder before she could escape the room. She ran for her life alongside the pool toward the lobby, a distance of about 360 feet, as Yolanda followed. After struggling with the entrance door and leaving blood spatters there, Selena entered the lobby crying and screaming.

"Help me. Help me. I've been shot. Lock the door,"[9] she cried. She told Shawna Vela, the assistant-manager, that she feared Yolanda would shoot her again. Vela called 911 and then, phone in hand, she knelt by Selena, who had lain herself down on the floor near the front desk, her green sweat shirt soaked in blood. Vela and Ruben de Leon, sales manager for the hotel, attended Selena in the lobby, one on each side of her. They later testified that Selena held onto her chest, arms crossed.

"Ma'am, who shot you,"[10] shouted de Leon?

"Yolanda, Yolanda Saldivar in room 158."[11] Then "her eyes rolled back," said de Leon. Selena never spoke again.

Emergency technicians arrived within 2 minutes of receiving their call, and after five minutes, transported Selena to a hospital four minutes away. They couldn't get an IV started because her veins had collapsed. Her heartbeat was about 20 per minute. EMTs discovered the egg-shaped ring, an ironic symbol of Yolanda's betrayal, still clutched in Selena's fist.

At the hospital, several transfusions and all other interventions failed to revive her. Selena was pronounced dead of cardiac arrest and loss of blood at 1:05 PM on March 31,1995.

Meanwhile, Yolanda ran to her van and held the gun to her head, thereby holding police off for over nine hours before she finally surrendered. In October of that year, Yolanda was found guilty of murder and sentenced to life imprisonment with no possibility of parole for 30 years.

Had she lived a few days longer, Selena would have celebrated her 3rd wedding anniversary and her 24th birthday, both in April. Instead, she was buried in a gown of purple, her favorite color. Beside her in the coffin lay her cherished white roses.

Mourners traveled to Corpus Christi by the hundreds to honor the woman who lit a beacon for Latinos and held it high. Flowers and notes from adoring and grieving fans covered the fence around her little house on Bloomington Street. Another shrine emerged at Selena Etc. boutique. Another appeared at the Days Inn where she was murdered. Her albums sold out completely. Songs were written in her honor and tribute performances took place in the ensuing months and years. Jennifer Lopez starred in a movie based on her life.

An award-winning album came out in the summer of 1995. The beautiful *Dreaming of You*, intended to be her crossover album for the English market, didn't have the quantity of English language songs required for the album. Just as Selena's life was unfinished, so was the English CD. Regardless, it is a lovely album. The title song, a love song, rendered with great heart and passion, is sung in English, as is the beguiling, "I Could Fall in Love," as well as "Missing My Baby," and "I'm Getting Used to You." Some of her best Spanish pieces such as "Tu Solo Tu," are included. This tragic mariachi selection demonstrates the richness of emotion she could impart with her voice. Selena had wanted to record an entire album of mariachi songs.

Suzette said on the spoken liner notes for the album that Selena "drove us crazy," with her practicing, "over and over," "El Toro Relajo." It was a hard song to sing, and she wanted to get it right. And now, Suzette says, she loves to hear the "Crazy Bull" song on the album; that she loves all the songs. "Each one of them is special to me." Selena was at the top of her game. Listening to the spoken liner notes on the *Dreaming of You* CD, it's heartwarming to hear members of her family praising Selena, the person, the voice, the co-worker, daughter, sister, wife, and friend.

The Tejano singing star would never be forgotten in her home state. Two weeks after her death, on April 12, 1995, George W. Bush, Governor of Texas, proclaimed her birthday–April 16–**Selena Day** in Texas.

Located along a walkway on the waterfront in Corpus Christi, this is one of a series of tiles, hand painted by children in memory of Selena.

Selena's Marker is located in the Seaside Memorial Park in Corpus Christi.
Another Stone lies beneath this one with a Sculpture of Selena's Head and
Shoulders.

Mirador de la Flor, Selena's Seawall Statue in Corpus Christi,
Texas. Sculpted by H.W. Buddy Tatum, a Corpus Christi Artist.

Selena Quintanilla-Perez
Bibliography:

Arraras, Maria Celeste *Selena's Secret: The Revealing Story Behind Her Tragic Death*, Fireside Book Simon and Schuster New York, NY: 1997

Jones, Veda Boyd, *They Died Too Young: Selena*, Chelsea House Publishers, Philadelphia: 2000

Marvis, Barbara *Selena*, A blue Banner Biography, Mitchell Lane Publishers Hockessin, Delaware: 2004

Novas, Himilce and Silva, Rosemary, *Remembering Selena: A Tribute in Pictures and Words*, St. Martin's Griffen, New York, New York: 1995

Patoski, Joe Nick, *Selena: Como la Flor*, Little, Brown and Co. Ltd., New York, New York: 1996

Perez, Chris, *To Selena, With Love*, New American Library, a division of Penguin Group, New York, NY: 2012

Richmond, Clint *Selena! The Phenomenal Life and Tragic Death of the Tejano Music Queen*, Simon and Schuster Pocket Books, New York, NY: 1995

Quotes:

1) "You've got to…." "You're never going to…" Page 25 *Como La Flor*
2) "There were a lot…" page 57 *Como La Flor*
3) "…Something always just" page 57 *Como La Flor*
4) "If we got…" page 57 *Como La Flor*
5) "She is loving…" page 60 *Como La Flor*
6) "Selena, are you still…" pages 32 and 33 *Selena! The Phenomenal Life and Tragic Death of the Tejano Music Queen*
7) "Take a look around…" page 117 *Como La Flor*
8) "I love you…" page 158 *Como La Flor*

9) "Help me…" The Corpus Christi Caller-Times, Texas Vs. Saldivar, Saturday October 14, 1995

10) "Ma'am, who shot…" The Corpus Christi Caller-Times, Texas Vs. Saldivar, Saturday October 21, 1995

11) "Yolanda, Yolanda…" The Corpus Christi Caller-Times, Texas Vs Saldivar, Saturday October 21, 1995

More Notes – Selena

Page 159 - Birth and naming – Page 30 – Patoski, Joe Nick, *Selena: Como la Flor*: 1996, hereafter referred to as Patoski

The Quintanilla family lived and worked – Page 39 – *Selena! The Phenomenal life and Tragic Death of the Tejano Music Queen* – Richmond, Clint, hereafter referred to as Richmond

"the button accordion and the 'bajo sexto' – Page 11 – Patoski

Conjunto, which means "whole" or ensemble… – Page 37 – Richmond

Page 160 - She had a glowing personality – Page 38 – Patoski

They counted themselves as followers of the faith – Page 39 – Patoski

the main instrument – Page 40 – Richmond

Page 161 – "While Abraham scouted things out…" – Page 44 – Patoski

"I loved Lake Jackson because of the green grass…" – 33 – ibid

Selena saw the move back to Corpus… – Page 45 – ibid

Footnote – …Texas artists…singing Texas style – Page 48 – ibid

Footnote – Announcers…breezed effortlessly between Spanish and… – Page 52 – ibid

Page 161 - a tearjerker of a ballad, "Te Traigo…" – Page 50 – Patoski

…Freddie Martinez was sticking to Spanish – Page 49 – Patoski

Page 163 - …the extensive airplay of the song ("Oh, Mama") Page 56 – Patoski

The most important showcase (Canales TV Show) – Page 56 – ibid

He teased her in Spanish – Page 56 – ibid

Footnote: Cara's roster included… – Page 55 – ibid

Missing classes on Friday and Monday – Page 58 – ibid

Abraham pulled Selena out of Eighth Grade – Page 59 – ibid

Page 164 - "Dame Un Beso" was the first hit – Page 64 – Patoski

"Dame Un Beso" earned (Song of the Year) – Page 65 – ibid

Page 165 - Pete Astudillo , a Laredo singer...and Joe Ortega – Page 82 – Patoski

Page 165&166 - I was too busy watching A.B. and Los Dinos – Page 23 – *To Selena, With Love*, Perez, Chris, hereafter referred to as Perez

Page 167 - the Acapulco Vacation – Page 13 – Perez

    The pounding on the door... Page 90 – ibid

    Selena ... dreamed about her...wedding day. – Page 91 – ibid

    "Every time they came into the restaurant..." – Page 35 – Richmond

Page 168 - We named her Pebbles and took her on the road (the pets) Page 149 and 150 – Perez

Page 168 - A.B. asked her what she wanted him to write – Page 118 – Patoski

    She was a walking, talking Barbie – Page 118 – Patoski

Page 170 - I ended up installing glass block walls... – Page 207 – Perez

Page 171 - The blue Silverado truck was parked in our driveway... Page 185 – Perez

    "That's it. That's fast enough..." Page 176 – ibid

    Selena and I always listened to music on road trips. Page 168 – ibid

Page 173 - At times (during the frenzied time in 1994) everyone in the band was so tired... – Page 235 – Perez

    I really lost my temper...Page 237 – Perez

Page 174 - Yolanda couldn't explain herself, Selena told me...Page 252 – Perez

    Selena...was still very intent on recovering our paperwork...Page 255 – ibid

    Yolanda reached into her purse...Page 255 – ibid

Page 175 - I locked the truck and took the path Selena... – Page 259 – Perez

Page 176 - "Chris says it's too late..." Page 262 – Perez

    She screamed at the sight... – Page 262 – Perez

    Selena started laughing that great big laugh...Page 262 – Perez

    "I couldn't find my keys..." the telephone conversation – Page 263 – Perez

Discography:

Amor Prohibido EMI Latin, Miami Beach, Florida 1993, 1994, 2002.

Dreaming of You EMI Latin, 1995, 2002

Entre A Mi Mundo Capitol Records, EMI Music, Hollywood, California, 1992
Selena Collector's Edition EMI, 2007

Videography:

Selena Live: The Last Concert, Q Productions, 2003

Selena appears in *Don Juan de Marco*, a film with Marlon Brando and Johnny Depp, released a week after her death. She wears a Mariachi costume and lip–syncs to another's voice.

"Stars on Earth and Stars in Heaven"

The Silent Sisters' stories reveal that exhaustion due to relentless performance and travel schedules, though perhaps not directly causing their deaths, was certainly a brutal reality in their lives. Readers may agree that travel weariness affected each of them critically. Yet each pursued her career as if drawn by the magnetic force of destiny, both captured and enraptured by her profession.

For all of us, life is enriched by work: learning trades, honing skills, climbing hurdles, keeping to the path, and often ignoring the difficulties. We try to balance work and play in our lives. For the Silent Sisters, although they stood upon the threshold of more peaceful lives when death intervened, this balance had not been reached.

They sang their fates:

With the ironic title "We've Only Just Begun," Karen's velvet voice renders one of her first successes.

Patsy's "Why Can't He Be You?" alludes to her ill-fated love life and overlapping romances.

Cass sings of doing extraordinary things in the song, "Extraordinary," arranged especially for her.

With the spiritual, "Don't You Weep When I'm Gone," a young, healthy Ruby sings her own elegy.

Janis croons her torturous arrangement of "Little Girl Blue," a Rogers and Hart tune that describes her lifelong mood.

Selena's "Como La Flor," tells of love that withers and dies like a flower, too short-lived.

To Karen Carpenter, Patsy Cline, Cass Elliot, Ruby Elzy, Janis Joplin, and Selena Quintanilla-Perez:

Each of you traveled mile upon mile and memorized line after line to bring us your songs. You sang it all: classical, blues, standards and ballads, folk, rock, spirituals, Tejano, and country. You rehearsed, performed, changed costumes, took bows and gave curtain calls night after night. You dazzled us with your resplendent voices and pitch-perfect performances. You also contributed enormously to the historic flow of American songs.

Your creative interpretations and individual styles often collided with contemporary conventions, redefining performance standards and expectations—forever changing the world of music. Your artistic innovations influenced the crosscurrents of musical trends among your colleagues and successors over the entire Twentieth Century and into the future.

You are now *Silent Sisters* but your spirits linger in our memories and your voices resonate in the songs you left behind. Brava!

Conclusion: Stars on Earth and Stars in Heaven

The chapter title is taken from the epitaph on Karen Carpenter's monument.

"Karen Carpenter 1950-1983. A STAR ON EARTH - A STAR IN HEAVEN."

Photos:

Unless otherwise noted in captions, the photographs in the book are by the author.

Acknowledgements

Ruby Elzy and Cass Elliot had one biographer each. I borrowed heavily from their work for the stories here. David E. Weaver published *Black Diva of the Thirties, The Life of Ruby Elzy* in 2004 through the University Press of Mississippi. I appreciate his important book and the encouragement he has given me. Eddi Fiegel published *Dream a Little Dream of Me, The Life of Cass Elliot* in 2005 through the Chicago Review Press. I admire both authors and recommend both books.

I am grateful to all of the biographers who researched the lives of the six singers and wrote about them. I relied on their work in putting together my shorter, more concise profiles. The authors are listed and credited in the Notes at the end of each chapter.

I appreciate the telephone interview with Charles Dick, Patsy Cline's husband who lives near Nashville. He helped me to correct several flaws in Patsy's story, especially as regards to earnings, band members, and the Las Vegas tour.

I'm grateful to the staff at the Peachtree City Library, Peachtree City, Georgia. They have placed holds on many books for me, and sometimes the same book several times. Libraries and librarians are best friends to writers.

I'm forever appreciative of the literary and social sustenance from family and friends. Without other eyes and perspectives, this book couldn't have happened.

Thank you to the members of my writing group, "Writer's Circle" of Peachtree City, and some of their spouses who have read various drafts of the book in progress, especially Rebecca and Tom Watts, Ann Wright, Paul Lentz, and Pat and Chuck Cruzan. Their comments and suggestions have helped me to refine and order the book.

To Director Linda Hooper and members of the choir, *Music Alive!* – Thanks for letting me sing with you on Tuesdays for practice, and several times a year in performance. Together, we celebrate American songs on a continual basis.

Thanks also to my friend and fellow writer, Anne Webster, for her advice and assistance, and to my editor Lois Patton, who helped me get my sentences straight and made suggestions for improving the work.

Thank you to my companion, Jerry Watts MD, also a writer, who has read several drafts and offered tips along the way. Jerry traveled with me to the hometowns of all the singers, making the trips entertaining for both of us.

My son, a journalist, gave me my first computer and with great patience, taught me to cut and paste sans scissors. And when Jerry and I got lost in Los Angeles, Eric drove us, on his day off from the Los Angeles Times to the cemeteries of Cass Elliot and Karen Carpenter. And Eric designed the cover for this book. Thank you, Eric.

I've tried to honor the singers with true sketches of their struggles and triumphs. Any mistakes are unintended.

www.ingramcontent.com/pod-product-compliance
Lightning Source LLC
Chambersburg PA
CBHW051726040426
42447CB00008B/990